BEFORE *And* AFTER *The* WEDDING NIGHT

BY Grace H. Ketterman, M.D.

How to Teach Your Child About Sex

The Complete Book of Baby and Child Care
for Christian Parents
(With Herbert L. Ketterman, M.D.)

You and Your Child's Problems

You Can Win Over Worry

Before and After the Wedding Night

BEFORE *And* AFTER *The* WEDDING NIGHT

Grace H. Ketterman, M.D.

Fleming H. Revell Company
Old Tappan, New Jersey

Unless otherwise identified, Scripture quotations in this volume are from the King James Version of the Bible.

Scripture quotation identified PHILLIPS is from THE NEW TESTAMENT IN MODERN ENGLISH, Revised Edition—J.B. Phillips, translator. © J.B. Phillips 1958, 1960, 1972. Used by permission of Macmillan Publishing Co., Inc.

Library of Congress Cataloging in Publication Data

Ketterman, Grace H.
  Before and after the wedding night.

  1. Marriage—Religious aspects—Christianity.
2. Sex instruction. I. Title.
BV835.K48   1984   248.8'4   84–3333
ISBN 0–8007–1205–6
ISBN 0–8007–6222–3 (floor display)

TO
WENDY
AND
DAVID

CONTENTS

Foreword   9

SECTION I BEFORE THE WEDDING NIGHT

1 Family Myths: Everyone Has Hang-ups   15

(Establishing a Solid Foundation; Understanding Potential Difficulties; Does Saying "I Do" Make a Difference?; Echoes From Old Tapes; Grief From Old Guilt; A Strange Thing May Happen After You Say, "I Do"!; Premarital Counseling)

2 Psychological Freedom: Everyone Needs a Clean Slate   25

(Freedom From Unhealthy Inhibitions; Freedom From Destructive Anger; Generalizations That Kill; Freedom From Guilt; False or Neurotic Guilt; Freedom From Fear; Freedom From Anxiety; Ways to Deal With Your Worry; Freedom to Be Who You Are)

3 Human Sexuality: Everyone Needs Adequate Information   41

(What Is Total Physical Freedom?; Dispel Those Myths; Define the Purpose of Your Engagement; Define the Goals of Your Honeymoon; Now You Are Married!)

4 Physical Relationships: Everyone Can Be Successful   51

(Female Genitalia; Male Genitalia; Your Erotic Zones; You Don't Have to Hide; If the Bride Is a Virgin; The Groom Also May Need Care; How to Know When You're Ready; What Position Is Best?; The Climax; Oral Sex; Allow Time to Adjust Before Having a Child)

SECTION II AFTER THE WEDDING NIGHT

5 Growing a Marriage Is a *Learning* Process   73

(Marriage Will Not Alleviate Conflicts; Commitment; Giving; Relinquishment of Power Struggles; Changes; The Ability to Postpone Present Pleasure for Future Good)

6 Wisdom From God's Word   89

(Husband—The Head of the Family; Characteristics of God's Love: Provider, Protector, "Priortizer," Positive Person; Opposition to Male Role as Head of the House; Wives—the Role of Submission)

7 Spoiling a Marriage Is a *Simple* Process   97

(Physical Problems; Premenstrual Tension; Emotional Issues; Time Priorities; Communication Catastrophes; Unfavorable Comparisons;

Inferiority Feelings; Jealousy—Constructive and Destructive; Spiritual Spoilers)

8 Restoring a Marriage Is a *Building* Process   119

(An Understanding Heart; Truth Is Distorted by Emotions; You Can Rule Your Emotions; Sublimation; Forgiveness; Information About Needs; Patience; Excellence in Communication; Honesty; Grace— Unmerited Favor; Wisdom; Realism; Faith; Trust; Congeniality; Love)

9 Maintaining a Marriage Is a *Fun* Process   145

(Characteristics of a Fun Marriage: Surprises, Excitement, Activity Sharing; Frankness; Yearning; Freedom With Trust; Fun Is Remembering; The Fun of Silence; Spiritual Bonding)

Epilogue: My Prayer and Wish for You   155

FOREWORD

The incredible brevity of the story of God's Creation consistently intrigues me. Such a magnificent production described simply but clearly in less than two pages of the Book of Genesis surely takes the prize of the ages for its literary genius! In only a few sentences this marvelous story depicts the creation of man, and from his rib, the woman was formed. Only then does the story tell us that God pronounced His work to be "excellent" *(The Living Bible),* or in the King James translation "very good" (Genesis 1:31). The grandeur of all the mountains, the mystery of the oceans, and all the array of botanical and biological life were incomplete without a man, made in the likeness of God Himself. And even man was incomplete until God made a companion for him.

On a human level, the mark of a masterpiece lies in an understandable theme or motif repeated in similar but variable styles. This gives the excitement of exploring a never-ending adventure, always new, but also familiar and therefore comfortable and secure.

The ocean is, to me, an example of this type of masterpiece. Each wave is similar to all of the others, and yet each is unique in its size, force, and motion—unendingly different, yet always the same—rising, crashing, and returning to its base, peaceful and secure.

Furthermore, the tides repeat the more dramatic excitement of the waves—rising and falling with unerring timing and profound majesty. When I've watched the mighty waves breaking over rocks or sandy beach, I've looked for shells and other treasures the depths might leave for me to discover. But I was always disappointed. The waves, no matter how small or large, left no significant deposits. It was the slow but ponderous movement of the tides, imperceptible to my observing gaze, that left shells and driftwood for me to pick and enjoy.

It seems to me this marvelous example of one of the Creator's masterpieces is quite like the new days of a marriage. There are little whitecaps of delight, repeatedly rising, revealing their tingle of joy, and receding in silence. These are the anticipated repetitions of the discoveries of a courtship—the tender looks and smiles, the unexpected touch, and the words that are never said too often: "I love you!"

There are also a variety of medium-sized waves, almost building to greatness but staying short of that, just keeping the awareness of power alive. Such waves are extra attentions new spouses may give. A special meal that lovingly satisfies a hungry stomach; a single flower given with tenderness for no reason at all—the extra efforts that are not heroic but very special.

On the wild, rockbound coast of Maine, during storms, huge breakers roar out of the ocean, throwing themselves over those boulders in a mighty crescendo of power. Such magnificent waves seem to me to be symbolic of the essence of the best possible part of marriage—that of the physical joy of lovemaking. The ecstasy of this special gift of God the Creator to husband and wife is like the breakers, ever changing and ever similar. The God-given freedom to explore each other and oneself for the most delightsome means of giving and receiving joy and love is like the waves—similar, but always a bit new and unique. A different perfume, a new musical record, a soft candle, a different place and position, all create the excitement of the new and different. But the underlying sensitivity to the other's needs and feelings, and commitment to each, should never change but grow deeper every day.

Not as newlyweds but later, a committed couple will discover the symbolism of the tides. As disagreements are resolved, hardships shared and overcome, losses felt and grieved together over seasons of time, the treasures of deeper love will be found. This love will be so profound, so powerful, that the excitement of joys and shared experiences—even of the breakers of sexual intimacy—will dim. The tides of time are necessary for the discovery of such a priceless treasure.

In a new marriage there are so many waves to see and explore. Each spouse must keep the freedom to do this independently at times—always remembering to share discoveries with the other. And the other must listen and receive the shared excitement, big or little, just as the ocean receives the wavelets back into its depth.

Exploring together, however, can be an enriching experience, drawing both husband and wife together in increasingly comfortable bonds of intimacy and understanding. In today's Western philosophy of great openness and narcissistic independence, spouses may be lured into very troubled waters. Therefore, the need to balance separateness and intimacy is profoundly important.

As the varying patterns of each individual masterpiece of marriage find new balances, creating new waves, and deeper tides, harmony in marriage is formed.

In His original creation of Adam and Eve, God put the potential for an infinity of variations for each couple throughout time. He does not, however, form it by His power alone. God created the marble from which Rodin carved *The Thinker*. He made the trees from which the *Mayflower* was built to carry the Pilgrims to Plymouth. To form and finish these human masterpieces, however, demanded *persons*—willing to work and rework, to refine and polish, to fit and furnish the product assigned to them.

God imparted the raw materials of the love, intelligence, curiosity, and creativity of His own Spirit into mankind. It is up to man and wife, however, to use these essentials to refine and make unique their own masterpiece. Just as an artist's perseverance and inspiration must join to demonstrate his genius, so must each couple be committed to work out the masterpiece of their marriage. In no area of life is there such a need for commitment to creative excellence as in making a harmonious marriage.

Western society today, by focusing on specialties, has lost sight of the whole. In pursuing the elusive wavelets, people have lost the patience to await the treasures of the tides. If one's spouse fails to make him happy, he (or she) is lured to seek easy pleasure in a different spouse, or a transient relationship outside of marriage. One marriage counselor, I was told, said to a depressed older husband, "What you need is a new and meaningful relationship!" The desperate man found a new relationship and lost his wife of forty-five years. He forgot the tide in following a transient wave!

Newlyweds may not like to hear this, but it is important to know that creating a masterpiece involves pain. Carving and polishing marble demands friction, cutting, and discarding of imperfect materials. But the end product will be one for everyone to study and admire. A marital masterpiece, too, is certain to know pain—but ultimately it will indeed be a masterpiece of harmony.

This book will guide you who are new to the adventure of exploring intimacy in marriage to a straight and true course. It is meant to give you the tools with which to carve out your special work of art.

SECTION I

BEFORE THE WEDDING NIGHT

–1–
FAMILY MYTHS: EVERYONE HAS HANG-UPS

Establishing a Solid Foundation

Barbara and Alan began dating in their first year of college. They were serious about their studies and involved in many campus activities, but they found time to study together and saw each other often.

It was Barbara who thought of creative things to do with their time. A quickly prepared picnic was the time to drive out of town and watch a sunset. Early mornings were a chance to jog to a local coffee shop for breakfast now and then. Window-shopping and ball games cost almost nothing and allowed them to explore each other's likes and dislikes, their temperaments, and ability to cope with disagreements.

Gradually Alan and Barbara progressed from the distant rituals and pastimes of college dating to a genuine respect and liking. They found their times apart to be invaded with thoughts of each other and a longing to see and talk to one another again.

To the surprise of both of them, they discovered that they could disagree (and even argue with some intensity) and still respect and like each other. They increasingly shared their likes and dislikes, their attitudes and feelings. They finally knew they loved one another. That love continued through times of absence and misunderstandings.

As their friendship, with all of its exciting discoveries, grew into love, they became more affectionate physically. One day they realized that they needed to set some limits and make decisions about the extent of those physical expressions of their love.

Both Alan and Barbara realized that many of their friends were choosing to engage in sexual intercourse during their dating. They understood that birth control could prevent any unplanned pregnancy—and they were quite sure of their commitment to each other's love. It was tempting to go along with the crowd. It would have been so much easier to give in to their romantic wishes and feelings of passion—but they decided to wait.

They realized that relationships may change quickly. They both shared a profound respect for marriage and their families. Neither wanted to hurt their parents or risk losing their respect by becoming sexually involved before marriage.

Intuitively Barbara and Alan realized, above all the other reasons for waiting, that the biblical injunction against sexual intimacy before marriage was given for a reason—and that reason had their highest good as its center. They became aware that their friends tended to break up after a sexual encounter or two. They saw the beautiful sanctity of complete intimacy become sordid, embarrassing, or at best disappointing. They felt increasingly pleased with their decision to wait.

Their lengthy courtship was full of exploration of many activities, sports, and adventures. As they learned each other's likes, they knew how to give pleasure in so many ways—an unexpected card, a rare special rose, a little rock from the mountains, a shell picked from the seashore where each vacationed. They valued thoughtfulness more than money, and cherished each other for the many varied facets of their lives.

There were many tender kisses and embraces. Often they sat just looking at each other's eyes or quietly clasping hands. There was not a sign of stiffness or coldness in either. There was often, however, a deep respect for each other and the decision they had shared. There were dreams and imaginings of the day when they could, with God's perfect blessing, become truly one in that special physical intimacy. Sometimes they spoke softly of that far-off day, but often they dreamed together in silence—in moments of personal intimacy beyond words.

Even after their engagement, their commitment held firm. This commitment was further reinforced by the wise counsel of their pastor. He met with them regularly at their request, to discuss any aspects of their forthcoming marriage they chose.

And then that day came—their wedding day and most especially their wedding night. With the blessing of those most dear to them and the happy wishes of their friends, the two set off on their honeymoon.

They had no bad memories or guilt to mar the ecstasy of their newfound freedom.

Understanding Potential Difficulties

Barbara and Alan were elated to discover they could share physical intimacy as often as they liked, and they liked a lot.

Interestingly enough, even their extensive counseling sessions had not prepared them for the fact that sexual desire could end abruptly and without a discoverable reason. Soon after their honeymoon Barbara and Alan found this out.

It was Alan who first experienced the shock of that discovery. After an especially stressful day, he was relieved to sink into the sofa and relax. Barbara soon joined him, tenderly teasing, playfully seeking his attentions, awaiting his passionate promenade to the bedroom. To her surprise, he remained listless, disinterested in her eager attempts to arouse him. Not understanding Alan's reserve, Barbara felt hurt, then fearful, and finally angry.

She had heard of marriages in which wives were frigid and husbands, desperate for physical fulfillment, went looking for it elsewhere. But she, Barbara, was not that kind of wife! What could have gone wrong?

Alan, in turn, was also puzzled, alarmed, and frustrated at himself. Why could he not respond to this playful, loving bride? Afraid of seeming (or being!) unmasculine, he could not face the situation. He did not know what to do or say, so he pretended to sleep and thereby avoided the situation.

Alan and Barbara made it through that evening. Barbara

sensed Alan's chagrin and graciously acted as if everything were fine. But an unnecessary thread of doubt was caught in the tapestry of their marriage's masterpiece that portended serious trouble.

Had this couple known it, most people experience times of fatigue, illness, worry, or frustration that rob them of their sexual energy. Such a loss is only temporary, unless it is compounded by more anxiety. The worst communication gap of all is silence. Barbara and Alan, on that fateful evening, succumbed to the power of their doubts and fears and could not break through that gap of silence for a long time. This example illustrates only one of a number of important potential problems that all newlyweds will face.

In order to begin sexual adjustment in marriage on a sound basis, there are some basic facts you need to know. Some of these are physical and many are psychological. As you read these, sort out the concepts that catch your attention and focus on them. As you understand each idea, it can become your own tool for creating that special marriage of your very own.

Does Saying "I Do" Make a Difference?

Despite statistics to the contrary, there are many couples who choose to save the specialness of sexual intimacy for marriage. Such couples must develop clear values and strong self-control. Like Alan and Barbara, when a couple practices such discipline for months, or even years, it becomes a habit—a way of being and relating.

For a couple like this, it may be difficult to release those controls after their wedding. In fact, I heard a bride say this: "It was so hard to comprehend that simply saying 'I do!' in front of our minister and friends could make a difference. What had not been right for us for such a long time was now okay. But I had a hard time acting on that belief."

If you are a couple like that, please understand that you do not have to hurry! On your wedding night, *take time* to talk with each other, show affection in the ways of your courtship, and slowly move into the freedom of the marriage relationship. Do not feel hurried. Remember, this is *your* masterpiece. It cannot and should not be like any other! Whatever you have heard from any other person, book, or fantasy must be put aside. Explore, in your own way and time, the very best approach to creating your sexual relationship.

Echoes From Old Tapes

No matter how enlightened you may be intellectually, or how determined in your will, you may discover that old-time tapes are playing in your unconscious mind! Many children grow up with ideas that were never put into words. They were, however, powerfully portrayed by parents' attitudes, behaviors, and physical expressions.

A man I once knew had been married twice, and was then divorced. The major problem in both marriages related to his difficulty in becoming sexually aroused. Before marriage, however, he had been unusually romantic, and found it difficult to postpone sexual intimacy until marriage.

As this man struggled with the confusion and frustration of his predicament, he remembered his "old tapes." His parents had made light of his romantic escapades with girls who had a doubtful reputation, but they emphasized that when he was ready for marriage, he should choose a "good" girl. They especially taught him that he must show this special girl great respect and certainly should not compromise her values.

Without consciously thinking it, this man, as a youth, acquired the belief that sex was okay with a bad girl, but it was not permitted with the good girls he eventually married. Mistaken or forbidding attitudes are tragically inhibiting in the bedroom of a bride and groom.

Make an effort, then, to remember what you believed about sexual intimacy when you were a child. By recalling those erroneous ideas you, as an adult, can consciously discard them and come to know that sexual freedom is a priceless wedding gift from the heavenly Father Himself!

Grief From Old Guilt

While there are many couples who wisely save sex for marriage, there are many who have not done so. Whatever the reasons, they may have experienced sexual intercourse with one or more partners before becoming engaged and married to each other.

If such couples are fortunate, they have worked through their pasts, forgiving themselves and each other. They will also have experienced the unexplainable release of the forgiveness of God and become free of any guilt. They are free from their past.

Sometimes, however, that release has not been discovered. There may even be secrets that have never been shared with each other and never confessed and forgiven. It is common in such people that deep guilt gnaws away at them, robbing them of innocence, openness, and the fresh opportunity to explore the wonder of their sexual discoveries.

Whether they are guilt-free or encumbered by remorse, such individuals are confronted with a troublesome problem. What if the new spouse, dearly loved as a person, is not as adept or romantic at sex as that one from the past? Unfavorable comparisons are hard to change and can become a specter robbing the honeymoon of its sweetness.

If you are caught in this predicament, I strongly urge you to consciously think through that old relationship. Be grateful that you have found a spouse who loves you and whom you can love. Allow yourself, privately, to feel the ache of the small loss of that one enjoyable part of the old relationship, and then bury it. Complete your grieving, and then discipline yourself to never look back.

You will thus be free to explore and grow in your marriage and love your spouse as you probably never could have loved that other!

I recommend that you do not discuss those old experiences with your sweetheart or spouse. Working through those old feelings, burying them, and knowing forgiveness is a personal matter. Each person must be strong enough to handle some things privately and independently. I have seen some relationships needlessly marred by doubts and fears due to revealing events from the past.

Exception to the rule. The only exception to this rule (and then only after extensive thinking and counseling) is in the event of some unfaithfulness to your spouse after making a commitment to each other. Discussing previous relationships often is based on unconscious reasons and may be: 1) cruel; 2) an attempt to prove one's desirability; or, 3) an effort to get that spouse to help alleviate guilt. Be extremely cautious about this situation.

A Strange Thing May Happen After You Say, "I Do"!

For at least a decade or more, a great many couples have chosen to live together without a commitment to each other and their relationship. They have, in a sense, "played house" in an adult fashion. I have known a number of such couples who later did choose to marry.

In many instances, such couples have told me about a strange phenomenon. As "playmates" they have enjoyed each other. Their sexual experiences have been exciting and fulfilling. But after their marriage vows, a strange constraint descends on them, and they begin to develop a tendency to have hurt feelings and short tempers. For these couples, marriage has been painful and confusing, and they feel their playmate status was more satisfactory.

Whether or not you have been involved in a "live in" arrangement before marriage, I have some information for you. This is knowledge that is vital to the health of your marriage.

Believe it or not, we tend to choose for a partner a person who resembles one of our parents. The old song goes, "I want a girl just like the girl who married dear old Dad." However, the chosen one may resemble the parent of the opposite sex—that is, Bob may choose a wife who has the personality traits and mannerisms of "dear old Dad," instead of being like the girl who married Dad.

Blessed indeed is the bride or groom whose parents loved each other and their children unconditionally, were faithful to each other, communicated clearly, and made decisions logically. Such a young person will probably choose a life mate who will prove capable of similar maturity. They will have a better-than-average chance of making a masterpiece of their marriage.

All too often, however, parents are not so wise, and their marriage is not so harmonious. A young person living in this imperfect family is almost certain to experience his or her own conflicts and confusion with one or both parents. He or she is highly likely to emerge from those family conflicts with many unresolved feelings and unfinished struggles.

While those struggles seem to have been left behind when the young person leaves home they have, in fact, become fixed within him or her. Buried and temporarily forgotten, the pain and confusion seem to be gone. In choosing a mate, however, strangely, that young person is most likely to be drawn to someone who seems like that parent with whom the greatest conflicts remain unsolved. In the sweetheart, the more pleasing traits of that parent seem to be paramount, and unconsciously one feels the old pain to be gone and only the good to remain.

After marriage there is a mystical, unconscious flow of one's expectations, reactions, and very being into the roles of the parents of one's childhood. Though there are no children for some time, or none at all, the spouses fall into their mother's and father's characters and the strengths and weaknesses of those parents go into effect.

He tends to see and hear in her not just her own likeness and words but the echo of his mom or dad, whom she vaguely resembles. And she, likewise, unconsciously senses the shadows of her previous conflicts, flickering in the sights and sounds of her new husband.

Each bride and groom, then, is sensitized to certain looks, words, and actions by the events of their past. Their misunderstandings and hurts are rarely those related to the here-and-now happenings of their new marriage. These troublesome feelings are superimposed on all the pain of the past. Hasty overreactions to little problems are unconsciously due to the build-ups of those unhealed wounds from the past and the new issues that resemble them.

This is a complicated matter, but taking the trouble to understand and correct it can transform your marriage. How much easier it is to know and work on this issue early in your marriage, rather than allowing problems to compound problems for months and years!

You must, of course, think back through those painful early experiences. Try to understand what caused your parents' problems. Be sure that you do not blame yourself for them, but do try to determine any troublesome habits of feeling, reacting, or behaving that you may have developed from those times.

Remember that you are now an adult, independent and capable of choosing wisely and constructively. With care and self-discipline, break the old patterns and learn to explore your life in each new day afresh. Stop all negative, old expectations and form new patterns based on hope and love.

No matter how much your new spouse may remind you of your mother or father, remember to separate them. Just as you must extricate your self from your past, be certain that you keep the new spouse free from the old webs. Learn to communicate clearly, to understand completely, and to love tenaciously.

Premarital Counseling

One of the benefits of premarital counseling is the identification of danger spots in each of you. Those powerful old tapes keep playing on subliminally, and will create many difficulties until they are erased. Good counseling can help you do that.

In the last three decades or more, broken homes and damaged lives have created a whole generation of young people who have grown up without one or both parents. They have been deprived of a secure, loving model for a successful marriage.

If you happen to be one of those young people without a model, and with scars from neglect (or even abuse) in your childhood, you will need special help. I strongly urge you to seek Christian counsel. Through this and through prayer, you may find healing for those hurts and wisdom to create your own unique model.

When such healing is complete, you will be ready for the exciting adventures of complete love in your marriage.

Healthy sex is not *making* love as people so commonly describe. It is, in its best sense, *expressing* love. In no other facet of life, in fact, are there the intense exchanges of giving and receiving, pleasuring and being pleased, listening and speaking in love, that are intrinsic to sexual harmony.

It is not by accident that the Bible uses the relationship of the bride and groom to depict the intimacy Christ would have with His Church. God created Eve first as a companion for Adam. It was indeed not good for him "to be alone."

The blessing God places on this exciting aspect of life is the highest and best possible permission to be free of inhibitions and fears—free to love and explore all of your lives together!

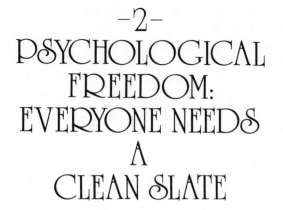

–2–
PSYCHOLOGICAL FREEDOM: EVERYONE NEEDS A CLEAN SLATE

Carolyn and Sally played together often. Their mothers were friends, and being together was easy and fun. They progressed over the years from playing blocks and balls to pretending school and creating doll families. One day Sally's mother stepped into the playroom to invite the girls to have a snack.

She was horrified to discover them playing with Barbie dolls and acting out adult sexual activities with them. That mother did all of the worst possible things. She evidenced her shock, scolded the ten-year-olds, and sent the playmate home. Furthermore, though she discussed this with her friend, she did not talk over the episode with either girl.

While this mistake is sad, the real tragedy of our world is the multiplicity of times it is repeated. Children have always been curious about sexual issues. They will explore their own bodies and those of their friends. And all too often parents' response to any and all such interests and experiences is a forbidding one. Sometimes there is severe punishment, but often there is only a frown or a look of disgust.

Casual comments and facial expressions can convey a wholesome sexual attitude or a condemning one. It is from such unconscious communications that we all form our adult concepts of sexuality.

Parents' treatment of each other is still another means of teaching sexual attitudes. When they are warm, tender, and respectful, children are indeed blessed. All too often mothers and fathers are rude, aggressive, or even abusive to one another. From such marriages emerge children who are likely to be fearful or aggressive. And as they grow, these children bring to their engagements and marriages troubled attitudes and behaviors.

Psychological factors influence marital relationships in all aspects—physical, emotional, and spiritual.

Freedom From Unhealthy Inhibitions

The unconscious part of people is a vast storehouse of such experiences, teachings, and observations. Out of that collection from our pasts come ideas and feelings that allow us to know that intimacy is safe, warm, guilt-free, exciting, and lovely.

On the other hand, of course, we may feel that intimacy is wrong, must be secretive, and is frightening if discovered. Such people generally have a constricted sexual life limited to the dark, under-the-covers expression.

Worst of all, certainly, is the belief that all sex is forbidden, bad, even sinful. Such teaching erroneously pictures that God forbids sexual pleasure and permits it only as a duty done in order to conceive a child.

Let me urge you to free yourself from any such negative, painful attitudes. These steps can help you to become free:

1. *Find some quiet, private time and recall all of those frightening, guilt-ridden experiences.* Think about the disapproving or threatening attitudes of the adults who were involved.

2. *In the very midst of those painful memories, imagine the presence of Jesus Christ.* Let yourself experience His loving concern about you. Tell Him everything. And ask Him for healing, forgiveness, and understanding. Ask Him how He feels about you and let yourself believe His

infinite yearning to comfort you and reveal His love and acceptance of you. Contrast His tender love and wholesomeness with those other attitudes.

3. *Search the Scriptures with an open mind.* Review the miracles of the Creation. Renew your understanding of married love through the Song of Solomon and other Old Testament readings. Think about the stated symbol of Christ and His Church as being like a bride and groom. You can hardly fail to understand God's perfect blessing and permission to enjoy your sexual life as a husband or wife.

4. If, by these procedures, you still cannot get free of the old negative attitudes, *find a counselor to help you.* Be sure to seek a person who has wholesome, biblical beliefs, or who will not, at least, belittle your own scriptural values.

Freedom From Destructive Anger

Millie and Kent were both strong-willed and outspoken. They often fell into intense arguments that left them tired and upset. Gradually these arguments left an accumulation of resentment. While this was troublesome during their engagement, it became even worse after their marriage.

Only a few weeks after their honeymoon trip was over, Kent and Millie were sleeping in separate rooms several nights a week. Their happiness was gone; they could no longer feel loving; and the last thing either wanted was sex.

Now let me hasten to explain that becoming angry is normal and universal. The many frictions and disagreements of daily living result in resentments and anger. We are all born with anger, so I believe that to be a gift from the Creator. Usually we do not bother to become angry with people unless they are truly important to us.

It is what people do with their anger that makes it a constructive force correcting problems, or a damaging power that creates difficulties. Ephesians 4:26 commands, "Be ye angry and sin not: let not the sun go down upon your wrath."

There are four steps I have found useful in obeying this order:

1. *Understand exactly how you feel and put that emotion into words.* "I am irritated." "I am frustrated." "I am absolutely furious!" Finding words to describe those emotions puts your mind in gear and will help you gain mastery over your emotions.

2. *Determine why you feel as you do.* Often the "why" is easy to define, but sometimes feelings emanate from old habits and are more difficult to trace. Stick with it until you are quite sure of the "why." This puts you even more in healthy control of your anger.

3. *Decide what you will do about the problem that caused your upset.*

4. *Put the plan into effect.* Be careful that your plan involves only what *you* can do. Avoid trying to make the other person do something because that usually ends in a power struggle. Be certain to keep your actions loving and constructive.

When Millie and Kent began to practice these steps, they learned to handle their problems quite differently. Each discovered that much of the anger was a cover-up for emotional pain the other inflicted. They found that most such pain was never intended, and that by expressing the very first twinges of hurt (rather than instinctively retaliating), they could avoid most angry clashes.

The anger that did erupt became a signal to separate into different rooms until they could think through the steps, and then return to discuss the solutions constructively.

When you are willing to develop a truly listening ear, cultivate a concerned heart, and keep an open, exploring attitude with each other, you will have moved a long way toward eliminating destructive anger. On the other hand, expecting criticisms, retaliating for offenses (real or imagined), or feigning indifference will fan the flames of little arguments into the conflagrations of serious battles.

Here are some suggestions for staying free from daily irritations and preventing seriously disruptive anger:

1. *Be willing to admit and describe the pain you may feel from each other.* Often oversights or misunderstandings cause real emotional pain. From early childhood, however, people learn to hide that pain, even from each other, by being angry. Avoid such an evasion and simply, honestly say, "Ouch! That hurt! But I know you love me and I don't think you really intended to hurt me! Have I, perhaps, hurt you? I certainly did not mean to." And then talk out what happened to create the problem, solve it, and get back to feeling loving again.

2. *Explore the meanings of each other's statements.* A slightly different connotation in a word can convey a very different sentiment. A prime example is the following statement: "You remind me of my mother!" Said in irritation about a parent with whom you may have some difficulty, that sentence can be a red flag causing pain and anger. If it is said in tenderness, it may communicate a high compliment. Whenever there seems to be an insult, check it out. If the insult is obvious, find out why it was given.

3. *Do not settle for hurt feelings and martyrishly suffer in silence.* Talk through any issue until it is resolved and the pain is healed!

4. *Admit to yourself, and interpret to your loved one, your unique areas of vulnerability to pain.* Warn him or her that slurs or jokes about such areas are likely to cause you pain.

An example of this comes out of my own marriage. My Pennsylvania Dutch farm family were up and working some hours before breakfast, and they needed a hearty meal.

My husband, from a small town, was not accustomed to eating much before noon, and he was constantly amazed at the breakfast menu of my family.

For years, he got lots of laughs from our friends by his accounts of those meals. I tried to be a good sport and halfheartedly joined in the amusement. One day, however, I became aware that this amounted to the ridicule of the people who were especially dear to me. I explained to my spouse that his humor was expressed at the cost of ridiculing the family I love, and I asked him to stop those jokes. Though he had not intended those stories as putdowns, he did respect my feelings and stopped telling them.

Other areas that commonly evoke a sensitive response are one's appearance, one's intellectual capacity, a variety of social habits, spiritual qualities, or personal traits. Be very open and honest with each other about sensitivity to insults and be careful to avoid the needless infliction of pain surrounding these issues.

5. *Learn to read each other's faces.* With watchful care and experience, you will come to recognize the often fleeting grimace of pain. Very quickly, the anger that covers such pain will supplant it, and you may only see the aggression. Never forget that, as lovers, each of you yearns to be beautiful to the other. You can either enhance that beauty—by kindness and compliments—or mar it by thoughtless rudeness.

6. *Make a firm commitment to always resolve all bad feelings—angry or painful—before bedtime.* ". . . let not the sun go down upon your wrath" (Ephesians 4:26).

Generalizations That Kill

In recent years there has been a growing storm of anger in our world that is categorical. "All men are bad—out to get you!" "All women are manipulators. They'll take you for all you have!" "All adults are stupid." "All kids are rude!" These are examples of the sort of global anger that flares about us regularly.

A few years ago I was honored to be invited to speak on a panel at a local university. Various professional women were asked to describe their particular careers and answer questions. I was scheduled to speak close to the end of the program, and I became increasingly horrified to hear one woman after another speak vindictively against the cruelty, rudeness, and unfairness of the men who had limited their success and abused them in other ways.

I felt alone and almost afraid as I depicted quite another aspect of a woman studying and working in a man's world. I had found men to be courteous, respectful, and helpful, as I ground my way through the rigors of medical school and practice. We make of our world, within the home or outside of it, very much what we put into it.

You each need to examine your beliefs. If you have mentally joined any of the popular groups who are angry at the opposite sex, please discard such an allegiance. Cultivate an attitude of understanding and love for people in general. It will not only enable you to love your spouse more profoundly but it will also make of you a more loving person!

Freedom From Guilt

There are many sources of real and fancied guilt for every couple today. Sexual permissiveness and promiscuity are a part of our Western culture. Few women and even fewer men are virgins at marriage in the 1980s.

Even within the Christian community, I find that increasing percentages of young people (and older ones, for that matter) claim to see nothing wrong with sex before marriage. They assert that if you really love someone, it is expected that you express that love sexually.

Stealing of boy or girl friends is a challenge to many young people and this challenge, tragically, is sometimes increased by marriage. The openly designed plans to woo away a certain man or woman from a committed spouse is all too well known to most of us.

If either of you young sweethearts has deliberately stolen the other from another person, you are at risk. You are most likely to feel highly insecure because you realize that if he (or she) was vulnerable to your devices, so might he be to another. And so, in fact, it may be.

No matter how carefully you may have glossed over your mistakes or sins, or how carefully you may have rationalized your schemes, your honest self knows better.

Such guilt must be dealt with. This guilt is real, and it is God's special gift to you—intended to prod you into honesty and love that transcends such actions.

Real guilt, as contrasted with neurotic guilt (discussed later), can be removed, and if you are to be free to love, you must unload it. Here is how to handle guilt:

1. *Admit to yourself and to your God that you are guilty and name the misdeed of which you are guilty.* I recommend real care at this point regarding confessing prior sins to your sweetheart or spouse. Seek good counsel lest you use that loved one as a dumping ground for your guilt. You may leave him or her with doubts and fears that may never be allayed.

2. *Think carefully about the reasons for your misdeed.* Perhaps you felt lonely and unloved and needed a friend. You may have grown up feeling competitive and needing to win at all costs. As you understand why you acted as you did, you can forgive yourself. Equally important, however, is your need to focus on constructive measures to fulfill your needs. Otherwise you are at grave risk to do other painful things in subconsciously trying to meet those needs.

3. *Seek and accept God's forgiveness for your sins.* His promises are plentifully spread across the Scriptures. The

first and second chapters of the First Epistle of the Apostle John are especially emphatic regarding God's forgiving.

4. *Once you accept forgiveness, put those experiences and even the memories away.* You may recall them if you are tempted to repeat those mistakes, *but do not dwell on them,* and do not carry that guilt about as a self-punishment. Christ took the punishment for all of our sins upon Himself, and we no longer need to carry it.

False or Neurotic Guilt

Little children have a natural curiosity about all of their world, and that includes an intense interest in their total bodies—genitals as well as noses, ears, and mouths. There are times when parents understand and guide this natural interest into wholesome sexual education.

At other times, however, parents like Sally's mother become upset and express shock and anger at such explorations. It is the parents' attitudes that create a false sense of shame and guilt. It is this guilt which creates the painful restrictions of the inhibitions already discussed.

Yet another source of false guilt comes from the family triangles that commonly become established among mother, father, and child.

Ned is an example of a corner of such a triangle. He was the oldest son of a very typical midwestern family. His father had to travel a great deal, and Ned was left as his mother's helper and confidant for days at a time. He felt very proud of his role in the family and became close to his mother. Periodically, however, Father came home and promptly resumed his authority as the head of the family. Ned resented his dad and yet needed and respected him. Ned felt that he and Dad had become rivals for Mother's love and attention.

The conflict this raised in Ned's adolescent emotions was never quite settled. His guilt over resenting his father (and even over his yearning for his mother's primary attention) went underground. In his subconscious being these guilt feelings rankled and kept him from the freedom and spontaneity he craved in his own marriage.

False guilt comes from misinterpretations and from unconscious feelings. Information and insight are sufficient to free you from such feelings of guilt, which are not based on any real wrongdoing.

If you are unable to grasp or resolve false guilt that is buried deeply within you, please go to a good psychotherapist for help. This is not a disgrace and is no reflection of your faith in God. It can help to free you completely from the chains of guilt.

Through misinterpretations, many "religious" people have been indoctrinated in unnecessary, legalistic restrictions. If you are one of those people, I recommend that you make a written list of all the *do's* and *dont's* of your training. Honestly and prayerfully study your Bible to check out God's authority about them. Be careful to read it for what it says, and distinguish that truth from the human commentaries and interpretations you may have heard.

Freedom From Fear

Love cannot be complete as long as it is contaminated by fear. When any relationship is even partially built on a foundation of real fear, it is shaky indeed. By its very existence fear implies inequality, in which one becomes the master or parent and the other the slave or frightened child. I know of no healthy engagements or marriages where these roles are played out.

Certainly there are times when the line between fear and respect is fine indeed, but you must know that line and keep consistently on the respect side if your marriage is to be made a true masterpiece.

There has been a popular saying that emphasizes, "Love never has to say, 'I'm sorry.' " If being sorry means you are afraid of the other's anger or retaliation, then I agree. But if, on the other hand, you recognize that you have hurt the one you cherish, I hope you will feel the grace of remorse and the desire to heal the hurt.

Only a few weeks before her wedding, Louise was visited by a photography salesman. For only a few dollars, she could have a picture to give to her future husband as a memento of these last days of their engagement. They had very little money, however, and Louise was torn by her wish to have that picture and her fear of Gordon's disapproval. Finally she purchased the coupon, but in her nervous anxiety, she allowed him to find out about it. He was indeed outraged, and lectured her at length about her foolish extravagance.

Their relationship was tormented for years by the fear that encounter prompted. Louise gave to Gordon the power to control her by his bullying ways, and the more she gave in to his anger, the worse he became.

Not only is fear fostered by a master-slave relationship but it is also encouraged through guilt. When one of you has done something really wrong, you are likely to feel guilty, and then fear being found out.

One couple I know formulated a very strict budget to tide them through a rocky financial time. Both agreed to follow the guidelines faithfully. The husband loved to fish, however, and he simply could not resist the urge to purchase an expensive rod and reel. He had it in the trunk of his car for days, fearful lest his wife discover his dishonesty. During these days, he was extremely kind and helpful, unconsciously trying to compensate for his failure to live up to their agreement. Only when he finally returned the rod was his conscience free and his fear relieved.

In order to stay free from fear that will mar your marriage, here are some rules:

1. *Consciously decide and work to avoid the existence of a master-slave or parent-child relationship.* This demands regular surveillance of your individual feelings, as well as the dynamics of your interpersonal communications and decision making.

2. *Keep your consciences clear.* Avoid breaking your own code of ethics or the agreements and vows between the two of you.

3. *Practice openness and honesty, and build the trust that must be the cornerstone of your marriage.*

4. Whatever it takes, *eliminate the kind of anger that overwhelms that loved person.* Bite your tongue, count to 10 million, jog around the county in which you live, but do not allow anger to control you or to intimidate the mate God gave you.

5. Always recalling your vows to love and cherish each other, *think through each disagreement and decision clearly.* Strength that is real is gentle, and true gentleness is strong. Work through each sensitive situation with the gentle strength and clear thinking that are intrinsic to mature love.

6. *Find each other's weakness, not to prey upon when you are angry but so that you can give support when it is needed.* Become aware of these tender spots and ask for the other's help when you feel insecure.

7. *Develop your strengths, just as you clarify your weaknesses.* There will be times when you cannot lean on anyone else, much as you need to. It is then that you will have to exert your own strength to compensate for your shakiness.

8. *Believe in and cultivate your dynamic faith in God.* His wisdom and love often flow through others, but He knows our desperation and will directly help us when we have reached that point.

Freedom From Anxiety

One of the gravest mistakes people make is that of attempting *to always be strong.* Men in our culture are so often cast in the role of protector, or the he-man image. Not only do men expect this of each other but we women demand it of them as well. Tragically, I have seen women who would even test or taunt their husbands to make them prove that strength.

Men, on their side, may expect their wives to prove their sexiness or some other role they desire. If their spouses do not please them such men may hint that someone else would be glad to do so. And many marriages are broken due to such threats being acted out.

Unreasonable expectations and blind attempts to measure up to them are certain to result in anxiety. Unfortunately, trust cannot coexist with anxiety. If your relationship is being built of such faulty materials, I suggest you throw them out and start afresh with each other on a more solid footing.

Ways to Deal With Your Worry

Sometimes anxiety or worry are the habits of a family. One or both of you may have been carefully taught how to worry. You may even believe that you must feel anxious about things in order to prove you really care.

Here are some helpful hints for unloading your anxieties:

1. *Honestly define what your expectations of each other are.* If you are unconsciously or deliberately expecting the other to fulfill some dream or socially constructed model, please give that up. Discipline your mind and attitudes to accept your sweetheart unconditionally—faults and imperfections included. Only in the warm climate of such accepting love can your spouse become safe enough to love you back.

2. *Cultivate your trust of each other, your commitment, and your special love.*

3. *Share your other concerns regularly.* As you verbalize worries about your job, your budget, your friends, or any other burden, you will find they becomes less ominous. Giving words to your feelings is the start of taking control over them.

4. *As you discuss your anxieties, break them down into smaller parts.* Don't budget for the next year when you are

desperately struggling with the bills for this month. Take only as much as you can handle now, today. Successfully coping with that will enable your experience to grow, so you can deal with bigger issues later on.

5. *Together, make specific decisions about all of your worries.* Write them down and decide who will be responsible to follow through.

6. *Do follow through!*

Freedom to Be Who You Are

Had Lorna and Andy known on their honeymoon what they painfully learned some years later, their marriage would have been far happier. They did not know that they were critical and condemning of each other. They really had intended only to help each other be better, more pleasing individuals.

Andy spent the ride home after a party pointing out to Lorna several social blunders she had made. He was able to make his points devastatingly clear, and she was reduced to tears before reaching home. He was acutely aware of her tendency to be a bit plump and could make her feel as if she were the freak at a circus.

Lorna, in turn, felt grave concern about her husband's lack of spiritual devotion. She had always felt particularly close to God through nature, and she began to hope that Andy would be closer to God. Perhaps, she felt, if he really walked with God, he would not be so critical and would become more loving. In many ways she tried to draw Andy into her world and toward her God.

Some years after their marriage, Lorna and Andy were vacationing with their two children in the lovely Hawaiian Islands. She especially reveled in the grandeur of nature so lavishly endowed with beauty. Andy, however, loved the cities and shops.

One evening, after the children were asleep, Lorna left their hotel for the sandy beaches so smoothly warm from the day. It was night and a full moon was just above the distant horizon spreading its soft light through the gently waving palms. White-tipped ocean waves were playing over the sand, teasing it out into the depths of the ocean. In the background a band was playing island music. No one was in sight, and Lorna was bursting to share this exotic scene, so novel and exquisite, with someone.

She returned to their hotel room and described the beauty of the island, asking Andy to join her for a barefoot stroll in the moonlight. Andy, however, was immersed in his book and frankly was tired of her endless attempts to make him over. His refusal to join her first stunned and then angered her.

In silence, Lorna returned alone to her beach. She sat in lonely despair with tears clouding her view and dripping on the warm white sand. She finally understood. Andy would not change— ever. He would never love nature, never revel in the feel of sand between his toes, never feel the clear freshness as the ocean washed away that sand. He would not sense the awe and wonder at the ocean's vastness or its tireless caressing of the land. And that was infinitely sad to Lorna.

What she discovered through her tears, however, gradually wiped them away. Andy's individuality did not make him a bad person. Nor did it mean he loved her less. Best of all, it did not need to diminish her joy. Her tears had momentarily crowded out Lorna's vision of God's creative wonders. And as those tears vanished, she again felt the indescribable wonder and joy of that moon-drenched scene.

As she burrowed her fingers in the sand, Lorna's hands unearthed a small rock. Holes had been drilled through its substance by ages of washing by the ocean's waves. It was rough and uneven. But that rock became the symbol of Lorna's new vow. She would accept Andy as he was, and she would accept herself as she was. Perhaps through each one's uniqueness, their marriage would become a masterpiece.

–3–
HUMAN SEXUALITY: EVERYONE NEEDS ADEQUATE INFORMATION

Having understood possible psychological hindrances to sexual harmony in marriage, you may now unload them. Freedom from such previously unconscious problems will prepare you to explore with joy and wonder the excitement of your new sexual intimacy.

What Is Total Physical Freedom?

Such freedom involves four areas of your being:

1. Your conscience is free from guilt or guilt feelings, and you have permission to sexually explore anything that does not offend or hurt your spouse.

2. Your intellect is aware of the facts about your body and that of your spouse. You know how to communicate your needs and feelings, and how to hear your spouse's needs and feelings.

3. Your emotional being is creative and joyful in expressing the tender and playful as well as the intense aspects of loving.

4. Spiritually the healthy couple accept God's blessing of their total relationship. They know that He created them, so they

rejoice in all of life, and that includes total sexual openness and intimacy.

During courtship, those who have chosen to postpone sexual intimacy until marriage have focused the expressions of their love on intellectual, emotional, spiritual, and activity sharing. As a matter of fact, one good reason for postponing the complete physical expression of love until marriage is to allow time and energy to focus on these extremely important facets of the relationship.

A young engaged couple I once counseled became intensely involved in having sex while they were dating. Their energy was spent and their time consumed by heavy petting and frequent sexual encounters. Due to some serious physical problems of the young woman, they decided to stop having sex and focused instead on exploring the many other interests of each of them. They talked a great deal, made new friends, and developed skills neither really knew existed. Only later, after their marriage, did they renew their physical relationship.

They were surprised to discover that they had hardly known each other during the period of their early sexual activity. Sex was so intense that it literally consumed their energy, and they sadly neglected the exploring of activities, intellectual stimulation, spiritual growth, and emotional sharing that are so essential to total intimacy.

I hope all of you couples, engaged-to-be or newly married, have been busy getting to know all about every aspect of each other's lives, because with marriage come many new challenges to be met and conquered.

What must be done in the weeks before your wedding? You need to prepare yourselves for a happy sexual adjustment. I cannot emphasize enough how vital it is that you talk together—and *listen,* as well. Talking out your fears and nervousness will dispel most of those painful feelings. Sharing your anticipation, on the other hand, will heighten it and prepare you for a truly fulfilling honeymoon. You should discuss any myths you may be harboring; understand the purpose of your engagement; define your honeymoon goals.

Dispel Those Myths

Sexual intercourse is a blissful "must" for the wedding night. I have already explained that for some couples, a sudden release from a lifetime of inhibitions is unlikely or impossible. Furthermore, the tension and fatigue of preparing for and getting through the wedding ceremony and the parties surrounding it may leave both bride and groom exhausted. You have the rest of your lives before you. Don't rush into your first and most significant sexual experience under adverse circumstances. Take time to get rested and ready to make this a positive and memorable event.

Sexual intercourse is a natural, exciting event culminating at once in total fulfillment. This is the belief of many young couples, and I want to forewarn you that this is unlikely. Certainly sex is a God-given, natural function, but complete, mutual satisfaction takes time, work, and patience to achieve. It can be very pleasant "work," but conscious effort and patient understanding are essential to its success. Many couples would have prevented years of marital distress and replaced that with great joy—if they had bothered to read and learn together how to make sex fun.

A bride should not expect to have an orgasm for some time. This myth began with the awareness of some physical discomfort due to the breaking of the hymen and the stretching of the vagina. True enough, the tissue that has covered the opening to the vagina may not have been broken prior to marriage. In many cases, however, due to sports activities, the use of tampons, or earlier sexual experiences, this tissue is already stretched or torn and the vaginal opening is adequate. Even when this has not happened, the groom may gently stretch the opening with his fingers, exerting downward pressure, and this will prevent serious discomfort. Using lubricating jelly and gentleness can prevent

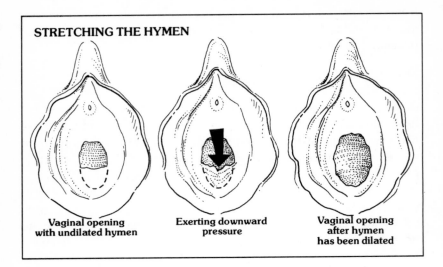

STRETCHING THE HYMEN

Vaginal opening
with undilated hymen

Exerting downward
pressure

Vaginal opening
after hymen
has been dilated

vaginal irritation. In the process of this dilation, the hymen may tear a little. Unfortunately, this is somewhat painful and there may be some bleeding.

The orgasm is a bell-ringing, bed-shaking experience. One beautiful young bride came to me for help because she had not been able to reach an orgasm. After several weeks of investigating the possible cause of such a failure, I asked her to describe just what she did experience during intercourse. She described a classic orgasm, but she had been misinformed. She believed that the entire bed would shake with the power of her sexual climax!

You "should" have sex a specified number of times weekly. Unfortunately, ours is a competitive society, and too commonly groups of people compare their personal lives. In order to prove their virility or sexiness, individuals may brag about their sexual prowess. Others who do not experience sexual needs or desires as frequently may feel inadequate or even fear they are abnormal. Avoid such comparisons. In fact, you should choose to escape such group discussion altogether. It is preferable, I feel, to keep some special parts of our lives private—not because of embarrassment or shame, but because of a sense of dignity and uniqueness. Have sex as seldom or as often as both of you feel you want to.

Sexual orgasms prove one's feminine desirability or masculine virility. Largely due to our sex-oriented society and too much talking and comparing, this myth has become commonly believed. It is the selflessness of your love, the honor you give each other, and the integrity of your entire being that confer upon you the highest degree of personhood. Sexual enjoyment is only a part, though an important one, of that whole.

Define the Purpose of Your Engagement

Especially in the weeks just prior to your wedding, find time to talk without pressure or hurry. There will be so many matters to attend to that you may lose touch with each other. Do not let that happen. Frequently find lengthy, relaxed periods of time to feel each other's presence. Use this time also to become verbally frank. Talk openly about your fears, hopes, and dreams for the future, for the present, for your marriage. Set some goals for yourselves and formulate plans for reaching them. As you develop this area of intimacy, include plans for a romantic sexual life as well. The more you communicate, the less your fears become.

Be certain that your commitment and responsibility remain clear. It is not unusual for engaged couples to become so close that they break their plan to wait for marriage to express their love sexually. Without protection against pregnancy, they find that a baby has been conceived before they planned.

Certainly engagement is a time for a steady unfolding of your physical relationship. Plan that growth carefully and prevent the pain of such an unexpected event. I am considered old-fashioned by many people, but I still believe in saving the exquisite joy of that first sexual completion for the honeymoon.

On the other hand, some of you will not have done that. The statistics clearly indicate this. I feel strongly that couples need time to adjust to each other in marriage before the arrival of a new human being into your home. You deserve to have a wedding that is surrounded by joy and peace—not hastened by the anxiety caused by a premature pregnancy.

Do use the latter period of your engagement to become much more free in expressing your love physically—but do so responsibly. Your decisions both portray and influence your character. And the strength of your character determines your adjustment in life.

Define the Goals of Your Honeymoon

All too often, a honeymoon becomes another vacation, busy and exciting, with sexual encounters squeezed into the general frenzy of activities. I urge you to plan more wisely. Whether you have only a weekend in a hotel or a lengthy ocean cruise, keep your priorities clear.

The main purpose of any honeymoon is to complete the foundation of your lifetime together. During courtship, you have explored each other's friends, families, interests, activities, and secrets! You have thought and learned together; you have decided on a church and have begun to establish your spiritual values. Hopefully, you have played, laughed, cried, and been angry with each other. You have, knowingly or not, been learning to work through disagreements and negotiate good decisions together.

All of these extremely important functions of your marriage need to be strengthened. And now, on your eagerly awaited honeymoon, is the time to complete your physical relationship. How you work out this special part of your lives now sets a course. Certainly this course can be changed, but you are wise to set it carefully now, so it can become increasingly pleasurable throughout your life journey.

Now You Are Married!

As we walked into the motel after our wedding, I felt a moment of pure panic. The thought that accompanied the anxiety was, *What in the world have I done?* I suspect most newly created brides, and grooms as well, have similar feelings and ideas. Just what have we let ourselves in for?

Preparation. When you settle into your room, perhaps your own apartment or house, or an elegant honeymoon suite, make it fun and tender. Express your nervous fears, laugh at yourself (but not at your new spouse), and talk for a while. You are now entitled, of course, to do exactly what you feel like doing, but I suggest that you not undress right away. Sit and talk and laugh together about the details of your wedding. The ring bearer walked about the front of the church? The flower girl forgot to drop the rose petals! The singer made you both weep a bit. Any special detail of this once-in-a-lifetime event should be savored, enjoyed, and tucked lovingly into your file of memories. Unpack your suitcases together and enjoy the fun of sharing toothpaste and space in drawers and closets. This is more than a ritual; it is the beginning of showing such considerations as who gets the top drawer, and what do you do when there aren't enough hangers in the closet? Be kind and generous without effusiveness or ridiculous insistence.

No doubt both of you have invested in lovely honeymoon nightwear. It is fun to prepare for bed privately, so you can dazzle each other with the surprise of your gorgeous pajamas and gown. One of you will use the bathroom and the other the bedroom. I must warn you new grooms: part of that blushing bride's face at the ceremony and reception is not her own. She will, in fact, take time to cleanse the makeup that has contributed to her loveliness. (And you may well believe she has succumbed to her nervousness and escaped out the window!) Do not worry. As a husband, this is only your first lesson in patience. Learn it well, for you will need it often!

Perhaps you, the groom, would like a quick shave, so you will present your best appearance. How can you manage that? You have probably never shaved in front of your sweetheart. There is something intriguing about watching a man shave, especially when he uses shaving cream. Even as a little girl, I watched in wonder as my dad shaved off those rough, dark whiskers. And I loved to watch my husband shave, but I'm not at all sure he appreciated that. Perhaps your bride, too, will want to watch you shave. If you are uncomfortable with that, you have a right to ask for privacy. But I hope you won't. This is another opportunity to grow in openness toward intimacy.

You both may dawdle and delay in your bedtime preparations on this special night. You certainly want to look and smell just right. More importantly, however, you may very well delay because you are uncertain about this new and special experience. What if you goof, seem dumb or awkward?

Be reassured! You are likely to do that—and so will your new spouse. And that, you see, is what love is all about! It's accepting each other's goofs and loving each other just the same. So relax; with a bit of humor, tell your new mate exactly how you feel. You are likely to end up laughing freely together and the tension will be gone.

Now you are ready. Once you have strutted about at length in your new sleepwear, I hope you will carefully remove it and just look lovingly at each other. This is your long-awaited chance to explore one another physically, just as thoroughly and happily as you have discovered so many other aspects of your lives.

There is no need to be shy any longer. It was for this very moment in Adam's life that God made Eve—for pleasure and for intimacy. It is for this time that you left your parents and made your vows to be committed to each other. Now investigate each other freely. Be as excited as you like. Her little freckle is cute, isn't it? You didn't know he had dimples there, did you?

No doubt as you look you will be magnetically drawn to touch. Now is the time to do that. To avoid rearousing old fears, start gently. Stroking and touching are pleasurable and will begin or greatly increase sexual arousal and desire. It is important, at this special point, that you use some self-control and progress slowly and considerately. If either grasps personal gratification and sexual release without tenderly helping the other to keep pace, it is likely to create disappointment or resentment. It may confirm the other's fears that he or she is inadequate or inept, or worse still, that you are selfish and inconsiderate!

–4–
PHYSICAL RELATIONSHIPS: EVERYONE CAN BE SUCCESSFUL

Before you progress further in this mystical adventure, you need to review or learn some basic anatomical facts. So you will know how vital such information is, I want to tell you a true story.

A beautiful, well-built young woman worked with me when we were both newlyweds. She was quite outspoken, and knowing I was a physician, she began to discuss her sexual problems. She was certainly not inhibited and seemed to have none of the common psychological hang-ups that often cause sexual-adjustment problems. As she talked and I asked a few questions, I learned that neither she nor her husband realized a basic fact—pubic hair may grow over the *labia* and it requires separation by the hands in order to avoid painful pulling of those hairs during intercourse. A simple bit of information transformed their sexual disharmony into pleasure. So let's chat further about your bodily structure, so you can be adequately informed and prepared for a satisfactory sexual relationship in marriage.

Female Genitalia

The special anatomical areas that are uniquely feminine are these: the breasts, which need little description in our explicitly breast-conscious society; the internal organs called ovaries, fallopian tubes, and vagina; and the external organs—*labia major, labia minor,* and clitoris.

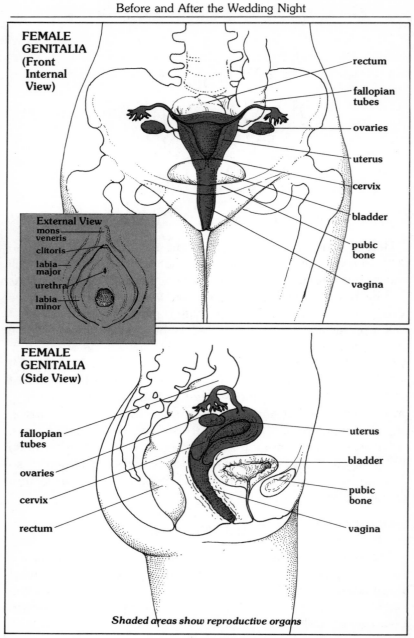

FEMALE GENITALIA (Front Internal View)

rectum

fallopian tubes

ovaries

uterus

cervix

bladder

pubic bone

vagina

External View

mons veneris

clitoris

labia major

urethra

labia minor

FEMALE GENITALIA (Side View)

fallopian tubes

ovaries

cervix

rectum

uterus

bladder

pubic bone

vagina

Shaded areas show reproductive organs

The ovaries are acted upon by and in return act upon the entire endocrine system of the body. They are the source of the eggs or ova that someday may unite with a sperm to create a baby. They are carefully protected well within the pelvis.

Lying over each ovum is an umbrella-shaped structure with fringelike projections. These are the fimbria and they serve, by the wavelike motion of those projections, to draw the ova up into the tubes. The fallopian tubes extend from the ovaries to the upper outer areas of the womb or uterus. These tubes are capable of soft, wavy motion that moves the ova on into the womb, where they are most capable of being reached by the sperm.

Neither ovaries nor tubes have much to do with sexual intercourse. It could be stated that ovaries, by their hormonal secretions, do influence female sexuality, and therefore are important to good sexual functioning. Many women, however, have lost one or both ovaries and still are capable of perfect functioning sexually.

The uterus is a roughly triangular-shaped structure. The base of the triangle is on top, and it is joined at both angles by the fallopian tubes. The apex of the triangle points downward and becomes the cervix or opening to the womb. The cervix, of course, is not pointed, but is a round tube. It extends down into the vagina a short distance while the womb itself lies in the pelvis, protected by the pubic bone. The urinary bladder is in front of the womb.

The cervix is very important in sexual functioning. Upon sexual arousal, its many mucous glands normally secrete a thin, serous fluid that lubricates and protects the vagina. This allows for smooth, painless motion of the penis during the thrusting and withdrawing movements of the final stage of intercourse. It is also the entryway for sperm to ascend into the womb. The sperm at ovulation, if not prohibited, unerringly find their way to the ovum, and one unites with it to begin a new life.

The vagina is a tubular structure with soft tissues lining it and muscles supporting it. As the bride learns to control those muscles, she can relax or tighten the vaginal walls to allow for greater sensation and pleasure during intercourse.

In a virgin there is a membrane called the hymen that partially covers the vagina. Almost always it allows for a finger or two to be inserted. This permits the use of tampons. Very rarely, the hymen is not open at all (imperforate hymen), or it may have several very small openings. In such rare cases there is a need for a doctor to incise this membrane. Without this surgical intervention intercourse would be impossible.

The vagina opens into the outer structures of the female genitalia. Lying immediately at the outlet of the vagina are two small, soft folds of tissue called the *labia minora*—small lips. They are, in fact, like small lips that protect the vagina and womb from any dirt or foreign bodies that could cause injury.

Over the *labia minora* lie the *labia majora* or large lips. These are rounded, firm, and on their outer edges there is skin rather than mucous membranes. There usually is some hair growth on them, as my friend discovered.

The *labia* extend forward and form a hoodlike fold over the most important female structure for sexual pleasure. This is the clitoris. It is a small (one-half to three-fourths inch long), firm tube that lies under the *mons veneris,* just over the center of the pubic bone and at the point of convergence of the *labia.*

During sexual arousal, the clitoris becomes enlarged due to the filling of special blood vessels and the tug of vaginal muscles. With adequate stimulation and motion, the clitoris develops strong, involuntary, muscular contractions. These movements spread into the vagina, reach a peak known as an orgasm or climax, and then subside.

The idea of a vaginal versus a clitoral orgasm is one that I hope will never trouble you. Most medical doctors feel there is one orgasm, beginning with the clitoris, extending somewhat to the vagina, but not so acutely felt there. Perhaps a variation in the intensity of the orgasm makes it more or less felt or sensed vaginally.

The *mons veneris* is a softly rounded protuberance over the center of the pubic bone. In women this is more pronounced than in men. It is mostly fat tissue and seems to have the function of protecting the clitoris. It is covered with hair, and when touched or stroked, begins to stimulate the clitoris to become engorged, erect, and ready for intercourse.

The amount and character of genital hair growth in women varies greatly. There may be almost none, or a quite heavy growth may be present. The variation is probably an inherited trait and has no other significance.

It is important that you both understand that sexual arousal activates the secretion of mucus from the many glands in the entire genital area. This secretion has a characteristicly strong odor. Unfortunately, I have heard that uninformed husbands worry about or even ridicule their wives because of this. Such attitudes are cruel and indicative of ignorance. I hope you husbands will never be guilty of such unkindness. And wives, be sure that your husbands know this from the start.

Male Genitalia

For reasons we do not know, the sexual organs of men are situated outside of the abdominal cavity rather than inside, as women's are.

Male genitalia include the penis, scrotum, testicles, and *vas deferens*. Located at the base of the penis, and surrounding the urethra, is the prostate gland.

We do know that the testes (common name for testicles) must be kept at the precise temperature they have outside the body. If they were as warm as the ovaries, the sperm would be destroyed. The Creator had a special reason for making them in such an exact manner, and that reason we do not know.

Each testicle rests in its own spot in the scrotum. It may move up and down but not from side to side. It is about the size of a large olive.

From each testicle there is a tiny but long mass of tubules (epididymis) that leads into a larger tube, the vas deferens. It empties into the penile urethra at the base of that structure.

The urinary bladder lies just under the pubic bone, and its

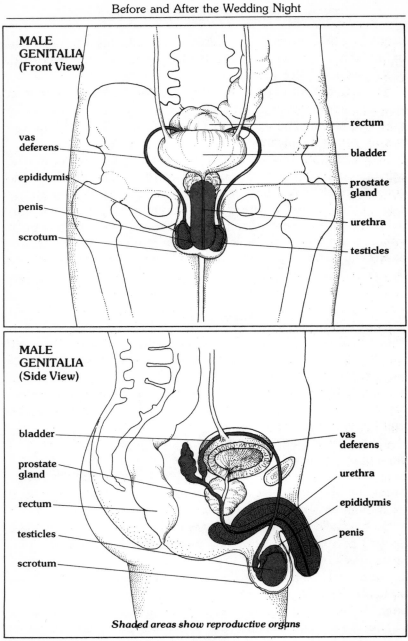

MALE
GENITALIA
(Front View)

vas
deferens

epididymis

penis

scrotum

rectum

bladder

prostate
gland

urethra

testicles

MALE
GENITALIA
(Side View)

bladder

prostate
gland

rectum

testicles

scrotum

vas
deferens

urethra

epididymis

penis

Shaded areas show reproductive organs

opening into the penis is called the urethra. A unique little valve shuts off that opening from the bladder, so that urine never flows out during intercourse.

The testes form limitless numbers of sperm and a thick fluid that carries them, called semen. Certain secretions from the prostate add to this substance. The semen is forcefully ejaculated during the male orgasm.

Due to the fact that semen takes some time to be formed, men are not able to have a second orgasm immediately after the first. When, as rarely happens, a man tries to force himself to ejaculate too often, he may experience severe pain. A few hours to a day or more are usually necessary for the renewal of a supply of semen.

Just as a wife's vaginal secretions have a characteristic odor, so does her husband's semen. One bride I knew insisted her husband see a physician because she found the odor so offensive. Do not be too sensitive. The odor is normal, and you will get used to it.

The scrotum is a fibrous sac that lies between the male's legs. The scrotum is usually darker in color than the surrounding skin and usually has a wrinkled appearance. There is some hair growth, but it is sparse. Pubic hair, and body hair as well, varies in men as it does in women. Some men have profuse growth of body hair, while others have very little. Unfortunately, some men still believe that quantities of body hair prove their masculinity. Your manhood emanates from who you are as a person, not how many hairs grow on your chest!

Your Erotic Zones

This lesson in anatomy was not intended to bore you but to inform you. A part of this lesson involves the familiarity you need regarding special areas of your bodies. These are called erotic zones, because touch of a special kind there can cause the arousal of sexual feelings.

In Western cultures, the lips and mouth are almost universally associated with sexual thoughts and feelings. Prolonged kissing and French kissing (in which there is an exchange of tongues into each other's mouths) are almost certain sources of strong sexual desire.

In other cultures, touching noses, ears, or other parts of the head have similar reactions. We know by this that erotic feelings are partly physical and partly a matter of training and cultural habits or mores.

Prolonged kissing on the neck is a common practice among young people and also may result in sexual arousal. Unfortunately, this often leaves a discolored area called in the slang a "hickey." The pressure against the tender capillaries in the skin results in some blood cells being drawn into the skin tissue. As these cells break down their coloring matter changes, and the area looks like a bruise.

The breasts, especially the nipples, are another source of erotic pleasure. Gentle fondling of her breasts brings a sense of fullness, and in fact, the breasts become engorged and larger during intercourse. For most women this enhances a sense of femininity and helps them feel sexually desirable. (While I hope each bride knows her desirability to the special husband God has given her, yet this added reinforcement is appreciated.)

Stroking the nipple will cause it to become firm and erect. The areola (the dark-colored area around the nipple) also will draw up and become darker in color. Many couples enjoy prolonged kissing of the nipples or even gentle sucking. This, in fact, can quickly cause a pelvic sensation of sexual arousal.

Massaging the abdomen, back, and buttocks also is likely to create sexual arousal. This is especially effective if it is done with short, gentle extensions of touch into the genital area. A few light touches may cause a clitoral erection faster than direct stroking. Likewise a few touches of the scrotum or penis can initiate the husband's arousal.

Touching the inside of the thighs and an upward massage reflexly cause movement of the testicles, which can be highly pleasurable. Certainly touching or massaging the penis are likely to readily cause an erection.

As you explore one another's bodies on your honeymoon, be relaxed. Let each other know when you experience pleasure. Telling your spouse what arouses and excites you will help him or her to pleasure you even more. And when you both do that, the mutual joy becomes beyond description.

You can now communicate in a new way. Certainly you needn't lose words, but sounds as soft as a sigh convey profound meaning. Guiding your spouse's hands or lips can be a creative language all its own. Develop your own language.

Do not be afraid to explore new means of sexual expression! Being creative can keep that sense of adventure alive. And that is part of keeping the romance growing. Just be sensitive to each other's needs and feelings and honest about those yourself!

To return to the wedding night: I urge you to *listen to your individual needs and feelings.* If you are too tired to have sex this night, please don't! It is important that you be at your best for this special, first event.

When you are ready, however, here are some ideas to help you enjoy sex from the very beginning.

You Don't Have to Hide

Certainly sex is private, beautiful, and personal. But some couples have intercourse only under the covers. This instantly prevents visualizing each other's loveliness. Some people even close their eyes during sex. What a waste! Seeing the other's responses is a big factor in communicating.

Try taking a shower together. As the water gently massages you both, you can add the thrill of touching, clinging, even having sexual intercourse there—another new thrill. In a secluded outdoor spot, on the floor by the fireplace, wherever you feel the urge and there is appropriate privacy, it's just fine. The world is yours!

If the Bride Is a Virgin

In discussing this book with a friend, she laughed at the idea that there might be any newlyweds who were not already sexually experienced. By statistics, I know she is only too correct. But I also know there are still a great many couples who have elected to wait.

Should that be your experience, there is a special technique you need to know. The bride should have a physician examine her before marriage. Very rarely, the hymen (the partial covering over the opening to the vagina) is so tight that it requires a doctor's treatment, as I described earlier. Also mentioned before, the husband can gently stretch the opening himself.

If you are successful in dilating the hymen adequately, you may wish to try vaginal intercourse promptly. If not, or if there is enough pain or bleeding to cause her some anxiety, I recommend that you wait.

Instead, try intralabial intercourse. With care to separate the labia and the pubic hair, it will be very satisfying to reach a climax without entering the vagina. The penis will probably massage the clitoris enough to bring your bride to orgasm. If not, massage it gently digitally until she, too, is satisfied.

Let me tell you, any frustration that may be yours due to such extra time and effort will be repaid a thousand times by your wife. She will remember your tender concern for her comfort and pleasure and will love you all the more for it.

Continue using K-Y Jelly and gentle dilation until the opening will allow the insertion of the penis.

The Groom Also May Need Care

When the groom has not had intercourse before, his penis, too, may be uncomfortable. This is especially true if he has not been circumcised. He will fare better if he uses a little K-Y Jelly. This is, in fact, one of the most important items to pack for your honeymoon and to keep by your bed. It is sterile, safe, protective, and soothing. Both bride and groom will benefit from its use.

How to Know When You're Ready

Surely you have recognized that I strongly recommend taking your time exploring and responding to each other's signals about arousal and pleasure. But you may not know just when you are both ready for sexual penetration.

Let me clarify that sexual intimacy has three phases:

1. *The arousal or foreplay stage.* This is the time that begins with the mental idea, the imagined or remembered feelings, and the wish to experience this pleasure. It includes all the touching, fondling, showering together, and exploring that I have described or that you can create.

2. *The active stage of penetration.* When you both are ready, the penis is inserted, preferably with the wife's help, into the vagina and thrust in and withdrawn successively until the stage of ejaculation and orgasm—the climax of expressing love sexually.

3. *The afterglow.* After the intense exuberance of the climax, there is a period of extreme peacefulness and relaxation. It is tempting to rush for the orgasm, then turn over and go to sleep. By giving in to that temptation, you will miss much of the meaning and most of the pleasure of your sexual intimacy. It is the ability to give and receive that is such a vital quality of maturity. In no area of life is that ability so tangibly expressed as in your sexual loving.

Take time to touch, fondle, embrace, and enjoy each other's bodies! As you learn more about the foreplay stage, you will discover the signs that you are ready for penetration.

1. She will have erect nipples that crave touch or brushing against his body.
2. Her clitoris will be erect and throbbing, magnetically yearning for the massage of his body.
3. Both of you will want to kiss intensely.
4. He will experience penile erection with a pulsating, throbbing feeling. Instinctively, he will feel an irresistible urge to insert it and experience release in orgasm.
5. Both will sense a physical reflex of needing and wanting to be so close that they are truly one.

For this shall a man leave his father and mother and be united with his bride—so they can be one flesh. This is it!

What Position Is Best?

Frankly, I believe too much attention has been focused on position during intercourse. If you remember the essentials in physical loving, positions will be several. Motion, relaxation, openness, and enjoyment will become the important factors.

As you reach the stage of active progress toward the climax of physical loving, it is most essential that you both are comfortable. A sudden cramp in the muscles of your back or leg can be severe enough to suddenly interrupt the most ardent sexual desire.

Probably the most common posture of this stage in loving is that of the wife lying on her back and her husband lying over her. Supporting his weight partially on his arms, his pelvis will be over hers, and his sexual organs will have ready access to hers. The wife's openness is most expressed in her posture—with her legs outspread and her hands fondly guiding her husband's penis into her labia and then her vagina. The use of her hands will help both spouses to feel comfortable, since her husband will need to have his arms available to support his weight. Furthermore, the wife can help the penetration to be gentle, slow, and positioned so that it is exciting rather than uncomfortable for her.

Remember that the wife's clitoris needs proper stimulation now for her to reach her orgasm, just as it needed fondling in foreplay in order to be ready for penetration. So be sure that both bodies are positioned in such a way as to stroke her, just as the husband's penis is stroked by her vagina. A pillow under her hips may elevate her body enough to permit this special pressure.

The penis needs to feel just enough pressure to continue the stimulation needed to allow the husband's orgasm. Often the penis and vagina automatically "match," and there is a natural sense of warmth and gentle friction. Sometimes, however, the vagina is larger and the penis smaller and there is not enough sensation possible to bring the husband to orgasm. The wife may help this situation with fairly little trouble. She can learn to develop her vaginal wall muscles until they increase their tone and tighten those walls.

By inserting her finger or a tampon, she can tighten the muscles until the finger feels gentle pressure. At first this may seem impossible, but with persistent effort, she will begin to sense how to tighten and relax both the external and the internal muscles.

Another way of strengthening these muscles is by sitting on the toilet seat with your knees separated. When you urinate, stop the flow of urine without moving your knees (which should be about two feet apart). After you get the idea of contracting these muscles, you can do the exercise anytime. With good muscle control here, you should be able to grasp your finger (inserted into the vagina about an inch and a half) very firmly. The benefits of this exercise for pleasurable sexual intercourse must be experienced to be believed.

An added benefit of this exercise is that it also strengthens the muscles that open and close the urinary bladder. Let me explain the importance of this. In women the urethra (the tube leading from the urinary bladder to the outside of the body) is quite short and the opening may be fairly large. The friction of the skin of the husband's penis may be irritating to the tender tissues of that opening. In fact, it is common for a bride to experience an infection of her bladder. Doctors call that problem "honeymoon cystitis," and it is painful enough to require medical attention. By exercising all of her muscles, therefore, she will learn to keep that opening much smaller and can prevent most of the risk of infections or irritations.

Some couples prefer to reverse the first position and have the wife lie on top of her husband. He may enjoy the touch of her breasts on his chest, and she may be able to find exactly the right position for her clitoris to be most beneficially placed. Some husbands, however, do not find the freedom to thrust and withdraw the penis in a way that is fulfilling to them.

Intercourse may be very enjoyable in a side posture. It takes a little maneuvering to position the legs in a comfortable place in order to allow the penis to be inserted. The position has an advantage, however, in allowing movement by both husband and wife that can help each to discover and enjoy the greatest sensation of pleasure.

In today's sexually sophisticated world, there are several other positions that may be assumed. One that has come into vogue is that of the wife kneeling and the husband entering her vagina from behind. This may be useful during pregnancy when the wife's enlarging abdomen makes the usual positions impossible. The problem with this lies in the loss of touch and pressure on the clitoris. The husband, then, will need to digitally provide that in order to bring his wife to orgasm.

The Climax

It is time to discuss the fact that you do not have to reach a climax simultaneously. One spouse, in fact, is likely to reach an orgasm first. Do not, however, believe that this must end your love session. In fact, it is important to change posture, renew the foreplay, and gradually bring the other to climax. Do not be reluctant to use your hands to digitally bring the slower one to a climax. Renewing the motions that you are learning will arouse your spouse and finally result in sexual fulfillment. This may take some time at first, so do not give up!

Let me emphasize that you should stay with each other until both of you reach a climax. If you give up, one or both of you will be likely to develop fears and feelings of inadequacy. Resentments may build, and eventually you may find that you are avoiding physical intimacy. Then you may be tempted to seek sexual release through masturbation, and eventually you may seek or fall into an affair.

Your love can make this physical aspect of your marital masterpiece just as harmonious as the other areas. God made you for each other—to enjoy, cuddle, play, and be intimately one. If it does take some effort, go ahead and make that effort. Surely you will be glad you did!

Oral Sex

I have been hearing some discussion of oral sex and its pros and cons. I was taught several decades ago that oral sex (called fellatio) was abnormal, and it was discouraged. In recent years, however, it has gained considerable popularity.

Coming from a simple, nature-oriented perspective, I have some personal difficulty feeling that oral sex is biologically "normal." Each part of the body was formed by the Creator for its own special purpose. We do not eat with our lungs or breathe with our hearts. Therefore it seems, simplistically, that sex belongs in the sexual area, not in the eating locale of the body.

Furthermore, it is possible for either spouse to have various oral infections. In fact, it is thought that the much-dreaded genital herpes had its origin in oral sex with partners who carried oral herpes or had "cold sores."

In spite of these personal biases, however, I would remind you that a sex activity that is agreeable to you both should be considered. If either objects strongly or finds it abhorrent, the other will understand and not insist. Satisfying one's own whim or need at the expense of the loved one's needs and feelings is not fair in the bedroom or in the kitchen—or in any area of life!

Allow Time to Adjust Before Having a Child

No matter how long or how well you have known each other before marriage, I assure you that you will have much more adjusting to do after the wedding. It is, therefore, most important that you avoid an untimely pregnancy. No matter how much you love and want children, you need adequate time to work out a solid foundation for your family by making your marriage strong and healthy.

You need straightforward, accurate information on birth control in order to safely take charge of planning your family. I do hope you will commit this special area of your lives to God's guidance and trust Him to guide you in just how and when to have your children. Here are the most common methods of contraception or birth control known today.

Coitus interruptus. The oldest form of contraception is called "coitus interruptus." That is a Latin term and it means that sexual intercourse is interrupted just as the husband is about to climax or ejaculate. The semen, therefore, is discharged externally and the sperm do not not have access to the ovum or egg.

The disadvantages of this method are two: 1. A man must be very skilled and well controlled to know when he is at the verge of ejaculating and must withdraw his penis when every instinct would be to insert it and climax within the warmth of his wife's vagina. 2. It is not a safe method because some sperm may be secreted no matter how careful the husband is, and a pregnancy could result.

Rhythm method. Another time-honored method of preventing conception is the avoidance of sexual intercourse during the days in which ovulation is likely to occur, called the "rhythm method." Most women ovulate sometime between the seventh day after and the seventh day before each menstrual period. A more exact timing of ovulation can be determined by taking your temperature and by testing the degree of acidity or alkalinity of the vagina.

Your doctor will need to instruct you in exactly how and when to take your temperature or test the conditions in the vagina. Do not try this on your own or from hearsay unless you are prepared for a possible pregnancy.

Many people have successfully planned their families with the rhythm method over a period of years but, likewise, many a surprise pregnancy has come about by its use.

The advantage of this method is its naturalness. None of the doubts or risks of medical contraception are of concern when the rhythm method is used.

The disadvantages include: 1. the rather prolonged period of abstinence from sexual intimacy that is necessary; 2. the loss of much of the joy of the spontaneity of physical loving; and 3. the uncertainty of effectiveness due to the irregularity of ovulation.

Barriers to the sperm. As you have surmised, the first two methods of contraception are effective through preventing the sperm from reaching the mature egg or ovum, thereby preventing conception.

The third method for preventing the entrance of sperm into the ovum is by the covering of the opening of the womb (the cervical os) by a barrier. Various ointments or jellies are inserted with a simple device that theoretically seals off the opening to the cervix. One of the more effective barriers is a soft rubber cup held in shape by a firm coil padded with rubber. This is called a "diaphragm" and must be inserted a short while before intercourse and left in place for some hours afterward. It is used with one of the many available spermicidal ointments.

I strongly urge you not to depend on spermicidal jellies alone to prevent conception. It is possible that they may not reach the proper place, or they may be injected too early and be lost through moving about.

The diaphragm is more than 95 percent safe in protecting against conception. It must, however, be carefully fitted by a doctor who is skilled in such evaluations. He or she must teach you how and when to insert it and when to remove it. You must be certain to apply jelly to the rim and in the cup before inserting it.

It is obviously a bit messy but is quite effective. Rarely there is a person whose anatomy makes it difficult to use the diaphragm, so if your doctor advises against its use, be sure to heed his advice.

The fourth barrier against sperm reaching the ovum is used by the husband. This method is called the "condom." It is, in fact, a thin rubber sheath that rolls onto the erect penis and catches the sperm when they are ejaculated. Obviously it is as frustrating to use these as it is to interrupt coitus. The spontaneous flow of the natural progression of intercourse to its joyful climax is interrupted by this method and may even make it difficult for one or both to reach a climax. Another disadvantage of the condom is the rare possibility of breakage. This can happen without the husband's awareness and an unplanned pregnancy may result. When I was in the hospital with our second baby, I had a lovely roommate who had just delivered her fourth child. She told me they had faithfully used condoms and this child was living proof that one had failed!

Prevention of ovulation. The surest method of preventing conception is the birth control pill. It is a hormone that prevents the maturing and releasing of the ovum or egg that normally occurs each month. It has been used in many parts of the world for over three decades, and has been approved in the United States for about twenty-five years.

There has been considerable controversy over the use of the pill. Occasionally it has side effects. After intensive study, however, most physicians agree that its complications are significantly less than the possible complications of a pregnancy itself, although in women over thirty-five, the risks do increase. This is especially true when women smoke.

It is important to have regular medical checkups when you are on the pill to be certain the dosage and type of pill are just right for you.

The IUD. This intrauterine device prevents the implantation of the ovum. It is a plastic coil that is inserted in the womb. Since there has been concern among medical authorities about the safety of the device, women who are considering using one should consult their doctors.

In considering what method of birth control to use, please be guided by the heavenly Father. Be sure to seek His direction to a competent physician, and follow the advice God sends through him.

SECTION II

AFTER THE WEDDING NIGHT

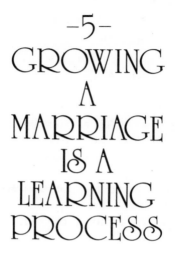

-5-
GROWING A MARRIAGE IS A LEARNING PROCESS

There have been many careful studies of the forces that mold human beings from infancy to old age. Various well-known researchers have defined certain stages of development and the periods of time in which they take place.

At this romantic and exciting time of your life, you won't care to read a lot of boring details about developmental psychology. Yet some ideas that relate to this important body of information are crucial for you to understand, because a successful marriage demands some level of maturity.

A great many marriages are not lasting even two or three years. That evidences a serious lack of enough adult status to work through even the initial adjustment. One young groom deliberately had a brief affair with a casual acquaintance to get even with his new wife. She had not totally pleased him, and he wanted to teach her a lesson. Unfortunately, she decided that two could play that game, so she, too, had a short affair. In only a few years, that marriage was broken.

In lover's idealism, it is easy to assume that such a tragic chain of events could never happen to you. But let me warn you—it can! And to be forewarned is to be forearmed. So this chapter will deal with some of the characteristics of healthy maturity, and how you may develop them in your own lives. You will need to apply them carefully in your relationships.

Marriage Will Not Alleviate Conflicts

Let me warn you to avoid such wishful thinking. Look at each other clearly, and face the facts as they actually are. If you can truly love each other, exactly as you are (or even "for worse" as the marriage vows clearly state), then you are ready for a commitment to marriage.

Carol was in the midst of the final preparations for her wedding. Parties and showers were all planned, and the house was crowded with gifts. Her wedding dress hung in all its splendor in her room.

Even in the midst of her excitement, however, Carol could no longer hide her anxiety. Donald was all too friendly with girls who worked in his office, and his enjoyment of an occasional glass of wine had become almost a craving for alcohol. As Carol pondered what their future might hold, she decided that the prospects were too risky. Three weeks before her wedding date, Carol broke their engagement, returned all the gifts, and wept out her grief over losing a dream.

Fortunately, she was mature enough to be honest. She faced the facts as they actually were, and acted on them. As disappointing as that was, an unhappy marriage, burdened with mistrust and habits born of character weakness, would have been infinitely worse.

Bob was worried about his fiancée's angry temper. When a plan did not turn out as she envisioned, she stormed and cried. Often she would actually stomp her feet and yell, in order to get him to give in to her wishes. On the other hand, she was playful, beautiful to look at, and was affectionate. Bob convinced himself that Sue would learn to love him enough to give up her anger. He was certain he could teach her to be more calm and reasonable.

During a long marriage, however, Bob was unable to make Sue change. She continued to have tantrums and to demand her way.

Marriage vows do not change individuals, and the more you try to change each other, the worse your relationship is certain to become.

Now if each of you is clear about your strengths and weak spots, you certainly may ask the other for help to overcome and correct those problems. You can encourage one another to build on the strengths, and enhance each other as much as possible.

Just know the difference between *helping* and *changing* each other.

Commitment

The ability to make a commitment. An honest commitment demands knowledge, trust, and firm decisions. The knowledge must include a reasonably complete awareness of your individual needs, strengths, and emotions. It must eventually include similar understanding of your fiancé or spouse.

Committed to what and whom? You must first be committed to your own basic honesty. Without that, there can be no trust, and then there is no foundation on which to build anything at all. Your own personal integrity is essential to your relationship.

Next, there must be a firm commitment to your betrothed. If you have not given up looking for other appealing partners, you are not ready for engagement, much less marriage. It is extremely important that you stop "shopping" once you have made your selection. You will find this tempting when your loved one's faults begin to emerge more clearly. If you cannot rationalize them away, you are most likely to try to avoid them, and then you will be tempted to think, *Betty [or Jim] certainly wouldn't act like this. Maybe I'd better dump this engagement [or marriage], and go back to her [or him].*

You will need to be honest if your knowledge is to be useful to you. When you are in love, it is easy to discount problems. You may convince yourself that his temper will become tamer after your marriage, or that her selfishness will disappear when she knows how important your needs truly are.

While there are a few situations when, like Carol, you really should break your engagement, there are more times when you should not! Certainly, once you are married, you must not consider such an option except in extreme circumstances. True, Betty or Jim would not act like *that,* but they are certain to act out in their own unique ways. There are, unfortunately, no perfect people. And if you should find one, he probably could not tolerate you!

Commitment demands priorities. Commitment to your spouse means you must say good-bye to your own family. Certainly you are to honor your parents, but the biblical command for that is matched by advice to leave one's father and mother to cleave unto one's spouse (Genesis 2:24). *Leaving* and *cleaving* are strong words—definite and important.

Calvin was extremely devoted to his parents. He and his father were partners in a retail business, and spent most of the daytime together. Calvin's father was strong-willed, and he controlled most of the business affairs. Frankly, Calvin felt a bit sorry for his mother, who was dominated by this powerful man.

After his marriage, Calvin found himself in an impossible situation. His obligations and feelings for his parents were often so strong that he did not know how to meet the needs of his bride, Debbie.

On her side, matters seemed even more intolerable. Away from her family and old friends, Debbie felt totally alone and, sometimes, abandoned. She began to insist that Calvin must correct his priorities, and when he failed to do that, she courageously took action. Debbie talked with her parents-in-law, explaining her position and the unfair tug-of-war she and they were having over Calvin. Through very hard struggles, Calvin gradually learned to *leave* his parents and devote his first loyalty to his bride.

Even devotion to old friends must take its proper position in your list of values. Ted was socially outgoing and had numerous friends. Even after his marriage, those friends, male and female, continued to expect him to spend extended times with them. On trips, most of Ted's time was consumed by calling or visiting old acquaintances. His wife, Anne, felt lonely and neglected, despite her best efforts. Ted and his buddies would become so lost in their memories and jokes, that they forgot Anne was around. Many times, Ted would play tennis or stop by friends' homes for long periods of time, forgetting his lonely bride.

Ted had not left his friends in favor of "cleaving" unto his bride. Finding the balance in valuing and cultivating good friendships, and yet keeping those clear marriage vows, *keeping yourself only unto her,* is the challenge of a good marriage.

Hobbies, also, can rob a marriage of its romance and intimacy. Dale loved to hunt and fish. His weekends were dedicated to finding the best fishing lakes and hunting spots and reveling in those sports. Of course, he had to find the best equipment, and that demanded trips to special stores or sports shows. His bride, Eva, at first saw Dale's love of these sports as evidence of his manliness, and she was certain that he would decrease those time-consuming jaunts after they were married. She knew that she would be such an attentive and exciting wife that he would want to stay at home with her.

Eva was wrong. That, indeed, is what should have happened. But Dale was insecure enough that he needed these sports to reaffirm his masculine image. As Eva began to ask more of him, he felt it as a power struggle rather than seeing her need of him. The more she begged for top priority, the less he would give. His hobbies had become Dale's mistress, wooing him away from a loving, disappointed wife.

The need for personal interests and hobbies is a valid one. No two people can (or should) devote every hour to each other. Each must retain and grow in his or her personal life. It is the prioritizing and balancing that make the difference. And such prioritizing demands choices and commitments all along the way.

Work can quickly become a jealous mistress. Perhaps one of the most deceptive forces in marriage today is that of the pressures of careers. Jobs are necessary in order to establish a home. But in today's world, jobs all too often become extremely demanding. In order to feel secure about your income or to gain promotions, you may find increasing demands on your time and energy. And often that leaves you with too little for each other.

Mary Ann was an airline hostess. Her job permitted the glamour of travel and an opportunity to meet many exciting people. It left her at home, however, with aching feet and little energy for sexual enjoyment. Richard had to struggle against his resentment and even jealousy about her work and its demands.

A few years later, Mary Ann quit work to have a baby. She was a good organizer, and found that her household tasks left her with time and energy to spare. She longed through child-filled days for her husband's adult companionship and anticipated their sexual intimacy with joy.

This period of time, however, had placed great responsibilities on Richard. He had to work long hours in his new professional duties, and came home at night exhausted. He felt little interest in sex at all. Fortunately, Mary Ann could understand her spouse and did not blame him, so they could work out their problem. She planned for child care occasionally, and was able to give Richard some time to rest and recuperate. After such refreshment, he, in turn, was more than happy to devote his time and renewed energy to his wife.

Be aware of the need to watch your time and energy expenditures. To maintain the financial security your family needs takes hard work and careful planning. Be sure, however, that you differentiate needs from wants. You cannot afford material luxuries if they rob you of the time and energy to love each other.

Your ultimate source of the wisdom and strength to make and keep these commitments is God. I hope that each of you knows Him and is dedicated to living in His Spirit. With His infinite power at your instant disposal, you cannot fail to make your masterpiece truly great.

Giving

Healthy balance in giving and receiving. The Bible clearly states, "It is more blessed to give than to receive (Acts 20:5)." And I know that the wisdom of God's Word is infallible. I also know that it says "more blessed," and that means there is some blessing, though less, in receiving. The ability to accept your needs and weaknesses, and to ask for help in meeting those, is also permitted. In fact, I see a grave danger when one spouse does too much giving. Let me explain.

Laurie was a generous, sunny person. She enjoyed surprises and planned extraspecial desserts for her new husband. She sacrificed without even realizing it, in order to give him an exciting gift for his birthday. Her every effort was made to please Brian. Where he wanted to go, she happily went, and the way he spent money she agreed must be the proper way. Laurie believed in submitting to her spouse, but she defined that as total slavery. His wishes became her commands, until she lost her own ability to decide or be a whole individual.

Finally, Laurie realized what had happened so insidiously but insistently to her marriage. It had become a one-way street with everything going Brian's way. Even when he had an affair, she wept in anguish but forgave him, and tried heroically to be an even better wife. She must not, Laurie felt, have been giving Brian enough.

In fact, the opposite was true. Laurie had, all unknowingly, encouraged a basically spoiled and selfish husband to become increasingly childish. He was unconsciously testing her out, as he had his mother before her, to see if she was strong enough to stop his risky, even cruel behaviors.

Giving and receiving sexually. In no other area of life, I suspect, is the importance of balancing giving and receiving more demonstrable than in sexual relations. The physical, emotional, and even spiritual exchange of pleasuring and being pleasured is lovely indeed in the sexual patterns of a truly loving husband and wife.

As one finds and bestows the unique caresses that build to the crescendo of sexual fulfillment, the other responds with evident joy, returning the pleasure and prompting more joy. Such joyful loving is reciprocated—the more you give, the more you will receive. What a wonderful interchange!

Giving and receiving gifts. In our romantic Western culture, gift giving carries great significance. This has, of course, been true throughout the ages and in all cultures. Ostensibly, the more valuable the gift, the greater the love of the giver. Now let me tell you a secret. That simply is not necessarily true!

Givers may, in fact, be exceedingly selfish, and they may give to gain admiration. They often give to manipulate or exert power over the receivers. People commonly give to assuage guilt.

Be careful to check your own motives in giving. And please be careful to avoid judging the other's reasons. You may become so suspicious or critical of the other's giving that he or she will give up, and stop trying to please you!

Let your giving, then, be focused on the selfless, thoughtful expression of your love in the symbol of the gift. Listening and observing will tell you when your loved one needs new socks or a single rose. Giving the practical gift with a creative flair can convey your love and kindle loving gratitude. Remembering the impractical, romantic giving can keep your relationship special and enhance its growth. A single flower is not costly, yet it conveys in a charming way your encouragement, appreciation, and love.

Giving help. There are so many jobs to do in preparing for your wedding and for your "forever after." All too often, these become burdensome and one begins to feel overworked or put upon. As marriage develops into its unconscious patterns, it is increasingly difficult to sense the imbalances in responsibilities, or even to define them.

It is, therefore, of utmost importance that you cultivate sensitivity to your spouse's burdens. A sigh or worried look may be your first clue that she is carrying more than she can manage. A need to stay up later, or bringing work home, can be the sign that he is under unusual stress. At such times, offer help and comfort—in that order! You may not vacuum the floor as well as she (though you can learn to do so!) or mow the lawn as easily as he, but do it without being asked. At least, do inquire about what you may do to alleviate the other's load.

Giving caring. How often we care about each other but show it in such poorly understood ways. A couple who are dear friends of mine demonstrate that exceptionally well.

Lynn becomes quite upset when her job is unusually stressful. As she should, she goes home anxious to unload her cares on her husband, Wayne. Being an intense person, she may cry or sound angry as she relates her woes. Now Wayne truly loves Lynn, but he feels no match for her strong feelings. In his awkward attempt to help he commonly says, "Oh, Lynn, don't carry on so! You're just making a mountain out of a molehill!"

Being a woman, I can understand why Lynn *really* becomes upset at that remark! Wayne, unknowingly of course, is belittling his wife's feelings as well as her problems. What she needs (but doesn't ask for clearly at all), is a sympathetic comment: "Gee! Honey, I don't blame you for feeling upset. That's a lot of pressure on you. Tell me more about it, or would you like for me just to hold you tightly for a minute?"

As you compare these two very different responses, try to put yourself in such a predicament on both sides. What would you like or need if you were hurting? And how could you respond to that need in your loved one?

It is just such empathy that can enhance the genuineness of your caring and refine its expression. Caring is not of use unless it is felt by its recipient as such.

Mature giving is free—no strings attached. Receiving is grateful, without a burdensome sense of obligation.

At some sacrifice, Elaine once gave to her husband a sizable sum of money. He was in a financial bind and needed it, so she withdrew the savings she had accumulated and handed him a check. He glumly pocketed it without a word of appreciation. At first, Elaine felt like responding in anger or tears, but she realized that she had chosen to give the money, and decided to ignore his ungracious lack of response. She had the right idea of giving simply and honestly—without expecting anything in return.

Now that enrichment of Elaine's maturity was well and good, but her husband, due to his own stress, missed a golden opportunity to reward her generosity with loving gratitude. Do not let that be said of you!

Relinquishment of Power Struggles

It was Friday evening, and both Flo and Steve looked forward to their date. They usually ate out together on that evening, and made plans for the weekend. Their wedding date was approaching and they had many things to do.

"Where would you like to go tonight?" Steve asked. And Flo promptly replied, "I've been hungry all day for pizza. How does the Pizza Inn sound?"

Now Steve had been hoping to have chicken, so he answered, "I guess that will be fine, but I was really craving fried chicken. Could you enjoy that?"

But the response came back frosted with some irritation, "Well, why did you ask me? I really want pizza!"

I will leave the rest of that conversation to you to complete in your own way. The essence of such controversies all too often lies in this question: "Who will get his [her] way?" All other facts become lost in resolving that one issue. And those other facts may be very important. For example, the cost, the location, the quality of food, and the atmosphere all become irrelevant. Who will win? That is the question.

To avoid power struggles, you must develop a healthy level of self-esteem and a strong belief in each other's love. Let me explain.

The person who unconsciously fears that he or she is stupid or inadequate, will set about in uncounted ways, likewise unconscious, to prove that is untrue. He or she will speak loudly, argue endlessly, and set out on many ventures in order to prove that he (she) is indeed intelligent, capable, and lovable. Unfortunately, the harder he tries to prove this, the less is he reassured, and a vicious cycle is initiated.

Sooner or later, such a person must recognize his own inner sense of inferiority and get rid of it. Building a healthy sense of self-confidence can then begin.

As each of you begins to recognize your individual areas of strength and weakness, you will be ready to stop power struggles.

Carl and Linda are a good example. He is unusually good at keeping accounts and budgeting. She is exceptionally skilled with blending colors and decorating their apartment. At first, Carl, wanting to be a capable householder, tried to manage everything. He spoiled her interior decorating by insisting on items that didn't fit. And Linda ignored the budget they had so carefully worked out, in order to try to correct his mistakes.

Fortunately, they realized what a lot of needless arguments and power struggles they were having, and they both agreed to back out of each other's specialties. Certainly they respected each other's wishes and ideas, but they stopped trying to control each other.

Whether your power struggles focus on sex, money, time, or any other area, they have this in common: the basic need for recognition and significance. The more you claim and believe in your own significance or "okayness," the more you will give similar recognition to your special loved one. Such respect is an essential part of your marital masterpiece.

Finally, keep your attention clearly focused on "What is right in this situation?" As you give up proving "Who is right?" you will find little need for such painful, fatiguing struggles.

Changes

Ability to adapt to change. One of the classic components of maturity is this special ability. Let me mention that such adaptiveness must not call for the sacrifice of your moral values. It does, however, mean that you take careful looks at your past and decide what you can bring from that into your present, and what you must discard.

Each of you will bring many unconscious habits and expectations from your childhood families into your new home and marriage. If you are not careful to think through these habits and your responses to them, you will be likely to build resentments, and begin to feel unloved and misunderstood. The outgrowth of these painful feelings could be emotional withdrawal, self-pity, and a wish to run back to Mom or Dad.

Financial changes. Before your marriage, each of you is likely to have managed your own money, without having to ask the other. This is especially true if you both have jobs and have lived quite independently. Such independence must change, though I hope it will not be lost.

I strongly recommend that you clearly formulate an overall financial plan that might go something like this:

1. Carefully total all of your necessary expenditures. Categorize them and write them into a budget. The problem here lies in the word *necessary*. Each of you will define this differently, but negotiate until you can agree on the inevitable *bottom line.*

2. Honestly total all of your income, and avoid holding out for the sake of that needed area of independence. (I hope this amount will be somewhat larger than the total expenditures!)

3. Decide together who will pay the bills, and how this will be done. Be sure to follow through at this point, and don't cheat by spending or charging more than you agreed upon.

4. From the extra money (again, I sincerely hope you have some!), you need to make three portions—one

should be a savings program that is insured and safe; another needs to be his to do with just as he pleases; the third portion should be hers, also to do with just as she pleases. The hard part of this is truly letting go of each other's personal allowances as well as honestly staying within them.

I assure you such financial planning will pay off well in personal as well as monetary terms. A husband whose wife's spending gets out of control is almost certain to feel either angry or inadequate. Neither of those emotions enhances love! Likewise, a wife who is unfairly restricted in her budget will feel controlled. She may rebel or ask her parents for supplementary income. Such a situation can set entire extended families at odds and create massive problems.

Changes in your financial planning will involve, then, *curtailing your spending, prioritizing your budget,* and *self-control in living up to your joint plan.*

Changes in your social life. Julie and Dennis had not been married six months before they recognized a sticky problem. Her parents had been accustomed to spending every Sunday with their own parents, as long as they lived near them. They now expected Julie and Dennis to devote every Sunday to them.

Since Julie and Dennis, as well as most of their friends, worked all week long, they had only the weekends to spend with them. They wanted some private time as well. Julie had to explain firmly that her parents would have to trust their love for them, even if they spent only one Sunday a month with them.

Tim loved to play golf. He had spent extended periods of every weekend with golfing buddies, and he didn't even consider changing those habits after his marriage. However, Ellen, his wife, began to resent his games, which left her not only alone but saddled with the week's laundry and cleaning as well. She worked full-time, too, and had no time for fun. Ellen and Tim had a great deal of changing to do!

Adapting to the changes marriage makes socially requires careful planning, just as financial changes do. I recommend these ideas:

1. Sift carefully through a list of all of your friends. Think about their qualities and values—and yours. On the basis of these, select two or three categories that you will form —those friends who will be close for life; those you will enjoy now and then; and those whom you will see only rarely.

2. Plan a social calendar, setting up times and ways in which you will cultivate the friends you both enjoy.

3. Always be open to forming new friendships, but do not become slaves to your social calendar. Keep plenty of time for each other.

4. Each of you will have some friends from the past whom you will enjoy separately. Discuss together how you will find the time for this without neglecting each other.

5. I strongly recommend that you restrict all personal friendships (not shared with your spouse) to people of the same sex as you. It is extremely easy in today's permissive world to allow unhealthy ideas or fantasies to slip between you and your beloved.

Changes in time. Just as each of you has spent much of your money as you pleased or needed, so you have expended your time. That, too, will need to change.

You may have loved reading a book all evening, without interruption. That needs to change. One hopes you will have some time for reading, but you need to communicate with your spouse now and be responsive to him or her. You will have some household tasks to take care of, and some sharing of each other's interests to consider.

The sportsman's wife may enrich their marriage by going with him sometimes—even if she reads or does needlework near him. The husband, on the other hand, may accompany his wife on a shopping or business trip of hers.

Be sure that you remain honest and open with each other. Do not, for example, insist on going with your spouse on a trip thinking you "really should," when honestly, neither of you wants that. You may both plan some enjoyable times apart and share them with each other, enriching your lives by extending your horizons. Now I admonish you to be exceedingly careful about this. You can grow so far apart that you lose touch.

The Ability to Postpone Present Pleasure for Future Good

This definition of *maturity* is one of the best I know. It applies to all of the decisions and problem solving you must face.

Whether problem issues involve money management, the many changes you must make, or prioritizing your time and social lives, this principle can guide you well. Some pleasures you may have to relinquish totally. Many of them, you may enjoy later. But always, you will know the adult thrill of thinking wisely and unselfishly, and planning lovingly.

The more you develop your personal wholeness through self-discipline, the more you will have to share with each other. Balancing your need with your mature independence is the essence of interdependence. And *that* characterizes a good marriage!

-6-
WISDOM FROM GOD'S WORD

Husband—The Head of the Family

Growing a marriage is no easy task, and it demands profound understanding and discipline. The best source of wisdom and understanding I have found is the Bible. I do not always comprehend it, and on the human level, I sometimes prefer to disagree with it. However, I am learning more implicitly that its truth is absolute.

In few other areas have I struggled with any spiritual issue like the one of submission. From my struggles I have distilled a few drops of wisdom I want to share with you. Perhaps from these ideas you will develop insights of your own that will help in creating your marital masterpiece.

"Husbands, love your wives, even as Christ also loved the church, and gave himself for it" (Ephesians 5:25).

Bill and Kate sat glaring at each other—fists tight, shoulders set, every fiber of their bodies screaming in painful anger. Kate had just described the way Bill had belittled her housekeeping efforts and her habit of being late for their appointments. The time was only six weeks after their honeymoon, and they were bitterly disappointed that their dreams of living "happily ever after" had been shattered so soon.

As I listened to their individual narratives, I soon detected that Bill had little understanding of his potential strength as a true head of the family. On the other hand, it became clear that Kate reacted to him as if he were her brother. She had argued and fought with him, trying to make him respect her more and treat her with greater consideration. Failing in those efforts, she was in my office, reporting to me (as she no doubt once did to her parents) how bad this person was.

So much of their heartache could have been avoided if they had understood the message of the Scriptures.

The balance in submission and Christlike love has, unfortunately, become misunderstood and negated in much of the world today. Even in Christian circles, these injunctions are often set aside as belonging to a remote era of time, hardly applicable to today's enlightened age.

Please indulge my supposing that if you *understand* these biblical commands, you can prevent or heal a mountain of troubles in your marriage. First, husbands, let me share with you.

Characteristics of God's Love

Provider. Christ loved us so much that He gave. You, as godly husbands, have the privilege of giving to your wives. Within the framework of your individual capabilities, you can provide materially for her—a secure home, adequate food, appropriate clothing, and the other necessities of life. Giving these gladly and proudly is an expression of your love.

You also can give her the acceptance and love that are as unconditional as God's love for you. You need to remember to show her your appreciation and pride in her efforts to be a good wife. Let her know regularly that you prefer her to any and all other women, offering her the gift of your recognition of her special significance and beauty for you.

The gift of your creativity in helping her at work, and planning for her recreation and play, can provide emotional luxury, far beyond the bare necessities.

Protector. Christ gave His life to protect His bride from evil and from her own sins. The mature, godly groom will, in case of grave danger, even risk his life to protect his bride. Bill was not faced with such extreme circumstances, but he failed to protect Kate from his own condemnation. Not only did he fail to protect but he actually attacked her in the area of her greatest weakness. The loving husband will help, encourage, and strengthen his wife's weaknesses, not hurt her.

Recently, a husband noticed that his wife was enjoying the flattery of a male friend of his. She was spending increasing amounts of time with this man, and focused much of her energy and attention on him. Randy, the young husband, was aware of the danger this budding friendship held, so he took action to protect his bride. Lovingly and firmly, he described to her the signs he observed of the attraction between her and his friend. He told her that he cherished her too much to risk losing her, and asked what she would do to correct the problem. Fortunately she was secure enough in Randy's love to stop seeing the friend.

Randy portrays another type of protection—that of a caring spouse who sees a potential danger and cares enough to put a stop to it. He was not jealous of his friend but protective of his wife and his own marriage. It takes tough love to stop a spouse who may innocently stray into a variety of traps that could destroy a marriage.

"Prioritizor." There is no doubt about it, Christ's love puts His Church and her needs first. And so will a truly loving husband put his wife's needs ahead of all other plans or values. He may need to distinguish between her real needs and her childish wishes or whims. The man who will *gladly* give up his Saturday golf game or Monday-night football on TV in order to help his wife, or even to simply spend focused time with her, will surely be rewarded by her grateful love for him.

Positive person. Surely Christ was (is) the all-time prize example of redeeming love. A loving husband will find some redeeming feature in every situation. His positive attitude will restore hope and secure the confidence of his wife. When dinner is ruined, the house a mess, and his wife in tears, he will thank her for her efforts, help clean up the mess, and think of a solution for dinner

—but only after he has comforted her and held her close. You may think that sounds unrealistic, but let me assure you that it is not only possible but is also an incredibly successful way to build your marriage—*your* masterpiece.

Using tenderness, healthy humor (which never makes the other the target of ridicule), encouragement, and above all, personal assistance in times of need, will express your positive attitude in love.

Opposition to Male Role as Head of the House

There are several reasons for the loss of the biblical concept of men as the head of the family.

Headship may become dictatorship. Out of weakness and insecurity, many men become tyrants. They rule their families with selfishness and exploit their wives shamefully. Understandably, wives rebel against such tyranny. Cruelty by husbands is a major disobedience to God's command to love as Christ loved.

Fear of responsibility makes husbands abdicate. In the last four decades, at least, boys have been increasingly raised by their mothers rather than their fathers. Due to World War II, many fathers were gone when their sons were born. All too few of these men returned, and those who did found themselves and their families quite changed. Divorces became rampant, and many children were raised by single mothers or, eventually, stepparents.

Young men raised in such families often carried heavy responsibilities prematurely. Their burdens were complicated by the needs of their mothers, who often ended up pampering their sons in order to keep their love and support.

Many young men reared in such families are tired of responsibilities and confused by the inconsistencies in their discipline. They enter into marriage, unconsciously expecting their wives to pamper them, as their mothers did, and they, frankly, are afraid they cannot handle the adult burdens of managing a household.

They leave many of those burdens to their wives and are surprised when the women complain!

Wives are afraid of (or angry at) men. Child abuse of the cruelest sort is increasingly common in the world. Little girls whose fathers or stepfathers have hurt them are certain to carry those intense emotions of fear or anger into their marriages. Such brides are likely to be overly dependent, creating extreme burdens on already insecure husbands. Or they may be unconsciously angry, setting up power struggles that destroy a husband's self-confidence.

Whatever the reasons that have robbed you men of God's intended position for you, please overcome them. By His power, you can. And I hope you can see the immense benefits to you and your wife when you do.

Wives—the Role of Submission

It has been increasingly difficult for young men to accept their position as the heads of their families in recent years. It has been infinitely more difficult to help women recognize the need for submission. There are several clear reasons for this.

Misunderstanding of the word submission. That term originated from the Latin. The prefix *sub* means "under." The main word *mission* is derived from *mitto,* meaning, "I send."

Most people believe the word indicates slavishness or assuming a "doormat" posture. No wonder women don't want to submit. But nothing could be further from the truth! The term, in fact, implies the greatest power God gave to His creatures—that of personal choice. Choosing to send my will under that of my spouse gives my husband the confidence to fulfill the role God intended him to take, and it allows me to develop a good sense of trust—the trust that is the essence of any lasting relationship.

Lack of trust. The hurts that one human being can inflict on another are infinite, and Western society these days is no exception to the rest of history. Boys and girls alike are unthinkably abused by the very people who should protect them—their parents. While abuse of boys also leaves its tragic scars, the sexual acts that are perpetrated on little girls leave them with a strange combination of fear, excitement, guilt, and anger. The pervasive weakening of trust is certain to make any tolerance for the concept of submission most difficult.

Not only is it abuse that weakens trust but neglect will do so, too, in a subtle manner. The father who is unconcerned about his child's affairs, who is often absent physically and uninvolved emotionally, will slowly create a father-sized vacuum in the life of his daughter. Almost worse than abuse is the total lack of communication, sharing, or intimacy that such indifference creates.

You can imagine the emptiness such a lack of a father creates in the life of a bride. She is likely to have a difficult time separating her need of a father from her need of her husband. Worst of all, she may fail to recognize her needs at all, making her husband feel unimportant and even useless. How can she submit, when she has so little experience in that area of life?

Husband fails in his responsibilities. Connie slammed the door and walked angrily up her quiet street. Her washing machine was broken, and laundry was piled high all around it. Peter had promised her he would fix it—five days ago. He did not want her to call a costly repairman, and he could fix it himself. If Connie reminded him, he accused her of nagging, and delayed the work even longer. If she said nothing, Peter seemed to forget the problem entirely. This situation had repeated itself with many variations throughout their short marriage.

Peter's behavior had marred Connie's trust, and the urgency of her needs had made submission impossible. He had not lived up to his own promises, and refused Connie any suitable alternatives. She had to choose to go against his wishes and call a repairman, or spend money at a commercial laundry. Their family budget was strained, and either of those answers created additional problems.

Wife's personal insecurity. As she lay across her bed, too tired even to cry, Myrna had to ask herself why she tried to do so much. She was working full-time to help her husband make the payments on their house and furniture. In addition, she was attending night classes to prepare herself for a possible promotion. She was sewing curtains for the kitchen, and trying to finish decorating the bathroom. She spent a lot of time keeping the house clean, the laundry done, and reasonably nutritious meals prepared. She and her husband, Larry, were active in their church, and tried to be friends with their neighbors.

The answers to Myrna's *Why?* lay in the lurking fear within her. She had never felt as successful or talented as her older brother, and from her earliest memories had pushed herself to the limit to try to measure up to his performance. The habit of overachieving had become so ingrained that it now was automatic. Her need to prove to herself that she was a worthwhile person drove her mercilessly. She rarely consulted with Larry about her choices, and if he tried to restrain her, she would anxiously argue with him. Her need to prove herself compelled her to perform rather than submit to his loving attempts to protect her by slowing her down.

Social and cultural pressures. Perhaps out of a collection of all of the above influences, and others, our Western society has pressured women to be independent, strong, and powerful. The right of a young wife to be a homemaker and mother has almost been taken from her. Frequently, I have young women timidly ask me, "Do you believe I *have* to get out and find a career? I can afford not to work, and I really prefer to make a nice home for my husband!"

All too often these earnest wives are surprised at my response. "Of course you don't have to have a career to fulfill yourself. The greatest job in the world is that of being a wife and mother!" God has a special plan for each life. Finding and fulfilling that plan the very best you can will bring the greatest joy you can ever know. If that divine plan includes a career, you can be happy in that. And if that career is being a homemaker, you can feel proud of that.

Be alert to a world that would "squeeze you into its own mould" (Romans 12:2 PHILLIPS). Carefully avoid submitting to such pressures rather than submitting in simple obedience to God's Word.

-7-
SPOILING
A
MARRIAGE
IS A
SIMPLE PROCESS

Today, as you dream of the years of married bliss ahead, you should feel great excitement. And that is exactly what you can have. Experiencing such joy, however, demands care and precaution. Healthy, growing intimacy demands as much work as growing blue-ribbon, prize roses.

It is unbelievably easy, however, to allow a marriage masterpiece to be ruined. Knowing some of the potential spoilers of your masterpiece will help you prevent their destructive work. Let me acquaint you with the most common threats to a great marriage.

Physical Problems

You are young now (at least most of you are), and you are likely to feel as if you have boundless energy. It is difficult to imagine feeling very differently from how you are now. But let me inform you that each of us has a measurable quantity of strength. When it is expended in one set of activities, there will be little, if any, left to spend in all of the other areas of your lives. Even sexual pleasure may become impossible if one or both of you are physically exhausted. Consider the following safeguards of your physical wellness to prevent the spoiling of your masterpiece:

1. *Budget your energy to allow enough strength for each other.* This will demand that you learn to work efficiently. Both on the

job and at home, you can find ways to plan and do the best work with the least energy expenditure. Keep your activities focused, so you finish each one as you go, rather than jumping from one to the other, and ending the day with nothing really completed.

Take short breaks every hour in order to fully relax your body, take a few deep breaths, and refresh your mind. Such breaks take only a few seconds, but they are remarkably helpful in renewing your efficiency.

Most jobs allow for longer breaks of fifteen or twenty minutes. Believe it or not, studies have proved that such breaks make work go even faster and more efficiently than grinding away without them. So enjoy yours, and experiment with the best use of them for you. A short walk may invigorate some of you. Others may need a quiet place to sit and physically relax. Try out as many variations as you can, and practice the type of break that most fully meets your needs.

2. *Plan your day.* One friend of mine found her energy level to be much higher when she planned her entire week carefully. Rather than working as hard as she could on Mondays and Tuesdays to get every household task done, she parceled these jobs out. By writing a reasonably flexible schedule, she balanced work, rest, and playtimes every day. She became excited about life, and looked forward to each new morning because that day held some special happiness time for her. She took charge of her time and made sure it included the joys of loving.

3. *Work together.* Many newlyweds have great battles over whose tasks are harder. When one is exerting herself to wash and iron, it can look like painting a wall is much easier. Now obviously, careful thinking about attitudes can reveal the fallacy in that belief. However, another answer to this problem lies in working together. You can both do the laundry and then share in the painting.

Above all, carefully try to ascertain and do what is your equal share in duties. But just as carefully, avoid keeping balance sheets. There will never be any two people who can, or should even try, to make everything come out to a perfect balance.

I like better my own philosophy, which is to keep my love and energy levels high; give freely of both all I have to give; enjoy the giving itself (loving, of course, *is* giving); and then mentally let go of each day. Keeping books on your spouse is risky at best, and downright destructive at its worst.

4. *As you work together, take "love breaks."* It only takes a second to smile or wink at each other. It takes less than a minute to stop for a kiss or a hug, and loving words or good humor can make work fun.

5. *Watch your nutrition habits.* I know how busy lovers neglect good eating habits. In favor of other interests, they head for work without breakfast, stop for a quick-food lunch while running errands, and are understandably too tired to fix a balanced dinner before going out in the evening. Please do not allow such practices to become habits. Your body cannot create energy without proper fuel. So refresh your knowledge of healthy eating, and discipline yourselves to sit and relax while you enjoy your food. Extra vitamins can help, too, when you are in the midst of exceptional stress.

6. *Get regular, individualized exercise.* It burns up stress hormones, increases the circulation, improves the metabolism, and enhances the general sense of well-being. Some people seem to prefer jogging. Others swim; some do strenuous calisthenics; others jump on trampolines. Find the form of exercise that best suits your body and personal likes, and then discipline yourself to do that regularly—at least three or four times weekly, if not daily.

7. *Adequate rest is as important as exercise.* What is enough, of course, varies from person to person. Listen to your body, and heed its warnings. When your eyelids persist in blinking, and your eyes burn, you probably are getting sleepy. When your muscles ache from constant exertion, stop moving and rest. Balancing

activities (work as well as play) and rest is essential to effective budgeting of your energy.

8. *Do not ignore signs of physical illness.* Headaches, stomach-aches, and backaches can be excuses to stay home from work. They may enable you to avoid sexual intimacy without direct rejection. And they *can* be signs of true illness. By developing profound honesty, you will usually know what is the truth about physical aches and pains. If you are uncertain, see your physician. Do not neglect the signs that warn you some part of your amazing body needs repairs.

9. *Think "wellness."* The Bible is right: "As a person thinks in his heart, so he is" (my paraphrase from Proverbs 23:7). Some families, out of loving overconcern, focus excessively on bodily functions and dysfunctions. If you come out of such a family you may not even realize that this habit is a bad one.

Just as you need to listen to the signals your body sends that warn you to protect your health, so you need to forget your body when it is quiet. Do not count the number of times you use the bathroom. Do not look for irregular heartbeats or minor aches or pains. Any real danger signal will assert itself repeatedly. You need not search for it. Practice health!

Premenstrual Tension

This age-old nuisance is partly physical and somewhat emotional, so I am choosing to give it the special significance I feel it deserves.

Many young women today—I suspect in pursuit of absolute equality with men—deny the impact of this entity. Such denial does not, however, negate the facts. For nearly forty years (less the time for three pregnancies), I experienced nearly every month a period of days in which the world seemed grim and foreboding. I felt as if ordinary problems had become world crises. There seemed no answers for them, and I could find no hope that there would ever be any solutions. I was irritable and short-tempered. Such was not my usual personality. I cried easily, and found it difficult to control these emotions.

The day after that menstrual period began—miraculously—all of those negative feelings, attitudes, and actions stopped. The change was almost as abrupt as turning on a light.

In medical school, I learned that there are valid, physiological explanations for those phenomena. The variations in specific hormone levels cause the body to retain fluids. Before each menstrual period, there is a rapid gain of several pounds of weight. This weight gain is due to the collection of fluids and is distributed over the entire body. The pressure such fluids exert on nerves and other bodily tissues accounts for the negative feelings just described.

Now let me hurry to explain that this information is not intended to give you young women an excuse for being grouchy! You can learn how to care for yourselves, as well as control your emotions, so you will not estrange your sweethearts! Here are my recommendations for dealing with premenstrual tension:

1. Get a good physical examination, and find out if you may need medication for a possible excess of fluid retention.

2. Explain, or ask your doctor to explain to your husband, what this is all about.

3. Ask your husband for understanding and patience during these difficult days. It is especially helpful, for example, not to plan trips or exceptionally tiring projects during those days unless absolutely necessary.

4. Psychologically, submit to the inevitability of this. There are some things you can do, and I'll tell you those next; but the very bottom line of this is that some disquieting feelings are going to assail you every month! Stop fighting and trying to deny them, and accept the facts.

5. Here's what you can do. *Plan your work schedule around your calendar.* Make as little stress for yourself as you possibly can on those days. *Don't stay in bed,* but lie down and prop up your feet now and then. *Avoid salt,* which tends to make you retain even more fluids. *Drink plenty of water and a little coffee or tea,* which serve as diuretics—substances that help us to excrete fluids.

Consciously discipline your mind to remember that the apparent grimness you *feel* is not a fact. Postpone thoughts about how terrible life, or your boss, or your spouse, is until the following week.

Now, young husbands or sweethearts, please do not use this information wrongly. You may discount all of your wife's tender emotions or concerns as being due to her menstrual cycle. Such an attitude will spoil her trust in you very quickly. You cannot afford such a luxury!

You men need to find that exquisitely fine balance between empathy and absenting yourselves. There are times when your wife will need to be alone to simply wait out her moods. At other times, she will crave your understanding and may cry on your shoulder. At yet other times, she may need your strength, firmly reminding her that this, too, will pass, and she will feel better.

Most women would appreciate this kind of response from their husbands—said with tenderness and understanding: "Darling, you're not quite yourself today, and I know it's that time of the month. I've just been thinking of how fortunate I am that I don't have to go through that, but I do care that you have to. I'll take care of the dishes and laundry this evening while you take it easy for a while. If there's anything else I can do, please tell me, because you do so much for me, and I'd like to do something special for you!"

Such awareness, expressed through words, feelings, and actions, will lift almost any wife out of the despair of those days—at least partially! And I know it will give you an even closer bond at that time with your new husband.

Emotional Issues

There are many feelings that are generated in and by every intimate relationship. Because of the intensity of the marital bond as well as the many complexities that spring from merging two different backgrounds, emotions are especially important to understand. They can become serious spoilers of your masterpiece. Let us discuss some of the more common feelings that can give you trouble.

Self-pity. If you grew up in a family that gave you much sympathy, you are likely to have learned to feel sorry for yourself. You may unconsciously look for slights and be needlessly hurt by little events. When one person does this too often, the other is likely to become disgusted, and may increasingly give real cause for hurt feelings. You can see how quickly a vicious cycle will build on such emotions, again, destroying the trust that is so essential to your love.

Anger. While some individuals are susceptible to self-pity over real or imagined hurts, others are quick to become angry. This anger almost always grows from lifelong habit patterns learned from childhood experiences and parental examples.

All too often, the angry person explodes quickly, intensely, and having dumped his emotion, feels fine. The recipient, however, is left with blame, guilt, hurt, and his/her own reactive anger. Over a period of time, such explosions and responses often come to a climactic point that can result in emotional distancing or even divorce.

Humor. Now healthy humor can often break tension, restore a sense of perspective, and help resolve problems. In other situations, however, it can subtly aggravate the issues.

One young husband seemed to bolster his own sagging ego by making critical comments to his bride. When she reacted with hurt or anger, he would laughingly respond, "What's the matter? Can't you take a joke?" Cynical humor can hurt as deeply as anger, and it is even harder to cope with, since its victim does not know whether to believe the hurt or the humor.

Do learn to laugh a bit at your own selves and laugh a lot *with* each other, but never *at* each other.

Worry, anxiety, and depression. These three crippling emotions can make your lives and your marriage unbearably heavy. Each merges into and tends to come out of the other, so you need to understand them, and learn how to control them.

Worry is a mental preoccupation with certain troublesome aspects of your life. You find your thoughts and energy recurrently turning to these problems, until they consume your energy, destroy your joy, and threaten your love.

Anxiety is a more physical reaction to stress, in which there is usually muscular tension with resulting aches throughout the body. There often is a rapid heartbeat, deep and heavy breathing, and various gastrointestinal symptoms. Along with these physical symptoms, there is a sense of foreboding or impending disaster. Usually the victim does not know what he or she fears may happen, or why he entertains such thoughts.

Depression is likely to develop out of chronic worry and anxiety. It involves feelings of anger, sadness, helplessness, and a vague sense of guilt and worthlessness.

These horribly negative feelings tend to be contagious. You can drag your spouse down into the morass of your worry without even consciously trying. And believe me, neither of you will feel like loving, because your energy will be consumed by such emotions.

Free yourselves from these crippling feelings by taking these steps:

1. *Define the cause of them.* While this is not easy, you can determine when the anxiety first appeared, and what happened to you at that time. Often a chance comment or transient situation may trigger such a response. Almost always, these current events are reminiscent of childhood experiences that created such responses.

2. *Clearly differentiate the past from the here and now.* As a child, you were helpless. As an adult, you have

strength to call upon. Earlier you were unaware of your options. Now you have the priceless power to think and to choose a course of action.

3. *Decide what you will do about all of the components of your dilemma.* Plan how you will carry out your ideas, and whom you may need to help you. This is a marvelous time to ask your spouse to be a sounding board, supporter, or active helper. Your plan can bond you into a wonderful team. Do make that happen.

4. *Follow through with your plan.* Do not allow the transient relief of forming the plan to deceive you. The anxiety will surely return unless you finish the job, and take care of all the details that involves.

Helplessness and excessive dependency. It is a compliment to need each other. Men in our society seem to be especially flattered by a woman's need of them. Books and philosophies have been based on the superdependency of the cute, helpless woman on her big, strong man. There are some relationships where those temperaments have merged in honesty and have built successful marriages.

In other cases, however, I have seen one or both spouses pretend a strength and a dependent helplessness that were far from real! Trust and love cannot be built on falseness, and I strongly urge you to avoid such games.

Your sweetheart or spouse is not assigned the responsibility for your happiness—only for loving and cherishing you. Happiness comes from within you, from your awareness of your own value, and from being productive.

I strongly urge you to be aware of your areas of weakness, and clearly ask your loved one for help. But do not allow your needs to overwhelm or burden your spouse. The balance in bearing one another's burdens (Galatians 6:2) and bearing one's own load (6:5) can be hard to establish.

Dishonesty. This is not, strictly speaking, an emotion. It will, however, prompt emotional storms if it is allowed to grow. When fear of your loved one's displeasure tempts you to conceal or deceive him or her, stop yourself at once.

Such fear reveals one of two special problems: first, you are doing something that is truly wrong and shameful, and you should be afraid because you deserve the displeasure; second, your spouse is too harsh and judgmental, perhaps bullying you, thereby unfairly intimidating you.

In either case, there must be a change. Wrongdoing will spoil any marriage, sooner or later. Undue anger and impulsive judging are equally damaging. If you cannot stop these by yourselves, seek professional counsel at once.

A healthy marriage must be an open one. There may be rare secrets that you avoid revealing in order to save needless pain. Such secrets must be exceedingly few, however.

Selfishness. When our children were small, they *occasionally* (!) got into arguments. I could tell such disagreements had reached their climax when one of them would pronounce emphatically, "Well! You're just *selfish!*" Children are quite accurate in defining characteristics of each other. They are not, however, very good at correcting erroneous qualities. All too often, the same can be said of their adult counterparts.

Selfishness is a common fault in many people, and it comes in many forms. Occasionally, those of us who take great pride in being unselfish are the most self-centered of all. We may, in fact, unconsciously try to lay a guilt trip on our selfish friends or spouses by flaunting our generosity. Do think carefully and profoundly before you issue a verdict of "selfish" to your spouse!

The selfish person, in my experience, is one who is deeply, unconsciously, and emotionally hungry. He is, for whatever the reasons, insecure and even fearful of something. It is acting out this inner fear of not having enough of something that we see as selfishness. Such a person is at least energetic enough to try to meet his needs—even though the method is wrong.

As they sat poring earnestly over their household accounts, Renee and Vern were a picture of anxiety. There was simply not enough money to make all the payments that were due. The payments for Vern's motorboat were only half-completed. He had decided to get a motor with greater power, and the additional payments were larger than he had expected.

Meanwhile, he needed a new suit because his promotion at work demanded that he dress up more. He was playing golf more frequently, and the cost of playing had increased. He needed new golf clubs, and his old shoes were worn a bit. As Renee and Vern faced the facts, it was *his* interests that consumed their incomes.

Renee had willingly turned over all of her paychecks to their joint account and had rigorously budgeted her own spending. After all, she and Vern were building a home and accumulating some security, so they could plan on a child in a year or two. She understood that Vern worked hard, and that he had been deprived of many things as a child. She wanted him to have what he wanted. So she continued to give to him and to give in, as well.

Secretly, Renee believed that if she gave enough to Vern, his needs would become saturated, and then he would begin giving back to her. This return, however, was not happening, and she was beginning to feel resentful. She finally faced the truth—Vern was selfish.

The secret of living successfully with a blatantly selfish person is to reverse the thinking of Renee (the giver). The more one gives to a selfish person, the more powerful he or she feels. Since he is inwardly weak and afraid, he loves to feel powerful. So he unconsciously thrives on others' generosity and takes advantage of them. He may have twinges of guilt now and then, but rarely are these heeded, because the habits of greed and its seeming security are too strong and too well hidden.

To stop the selfishness, let me suggest these steps:

First, clearly understand the dynamics of selfishness. This means that you learn about your spouse's childhood and the kinds of deprivation he or she experienced. Please do *not* play psychiatrist and try to make this clear to your mate. Just quietly understand and love him more because of that old pain of his.

Next, focus on the good feeling that accompanies generosity. If you have been the giving spouse, you will know that feeling well. Think creatively about your selfish partner, and how he or she can experience such a gratifying emotion. Of course! Through learning to give!

Then find a way to make that selfish spouse start giving! I recommend a firm commitment to this point, because it will not be easy. You have a lifetime of old habits to battle, so plan your strategy well. Asking to be taken out to dinner now and then, being clear about a gift you really want for your birthday, or requesting some specific help—these and your own innovative ideas will eventually prompt the beginning of giving.

Be sure to feel and express your joy and gratitude. Now this must be genuine and not too effusive! Furthermore, you will find it very hard to feel warmly when you have to work so hard to get the giving started. Remember, however, it is good feelings that are the best motivators. So do it—no matter what your inner thoughts and wishes are.

Finally, stop being so generous! Please don't go to the other extreme and become as selfish as your spouse was! Give whatever you choose to give, gladly and freely, but do not expect gratitude or any giving in return. The selfish person is not capable of much giving unless it brings rewards to him.

As you explore the changing of a habit of selfishness, I trust you selfish spouses will become secure enough to recognize that trait. When such awareness occurs, the entire problem disappears quickly. Few indeed are the individuals who really prefer to be selfish. Knowing that you have been, and understanding why, can prompt you to change.

For the selfish person, himself or herself, to change demands only this:

1. *Awareness.* And that has already been described above.

2. *Decision.* The commitment to grow and to stop being selfish is a turning point. It takes the efforts of painful

honesty, some introspection, and a great deal of determination.

3. *Tenacity.* Breaking any old habit is difficult, and this old habit has so many needs woven into it that it will be even harder to break than most!

4. *Help.* When anyone tries to break such an old habit, he is likely to become discouraged and want to return to old, familiar ways. If you find yourself so tempted, run to your mate or a friend, and ask them to encourage and help you.

5. *Enjoy.* The change from selfishness and insecurity to generosity and love will eventually reward you with real joy!

Time Priorities

Closely related to energy levels, and the planning that preserves these, is the need to regulate your time. I know of many young people who seem to believe they can take their marriages in stride. They do not see that a new spouse needs to change their life-style one bit.

Such an attitude is selfish, and it is based on a false assumption. Few indeed are the people who can build a great marriage on such a philosophy. The only value that should transcend that of your marital closeness is that of your relationship with God.

As your love, respect, and responsibility to each other grow, you will need to learn how to budget your time. Get up in the morning a few minutes early in order to have time for an embrace and a breakfast. Take time to call each other now and then—for no reason except to say, "I was thinking of how much I love you, and I wanted to tell you!" Stop off once in a while and find time to get a special card, or even to pick a wild flower, a colorful leaf, or any token that transmits an "I love you and here's a tiny conveyer of that" message.

Loving takes energy; it also takes time. So plan your time to allow for love outside of the bedroom if you want the greatest fulfillment in the bed.

Communication Catastrophes

So much has been said and written about communication that it may seem redundant to write more. In spite of such a wealth of information, however, individuals still fail miserably at this task.

Failure to recognize and share needs. Liz and Charles are a prime example of this point. Very soon after their brief honeymoon, Charles began to stay away from their apartment for extended times. At first, Liz attributed his absences to extra work, traffic tie-ups, and every logical reason she could think of, because she loved him a great deal and believed he loved her. At last, however, she confronted Charles about her worry that perhaps he no longer loved her and had a girl friend.

Charles angrily denied such a possibility and told Liz that she had no right to check up on him. He simply needed some time alone, he emphasized. Nevertheless, his interest in his bride lost its intensity, and even their sexual interactions became less frequent and more routine.

Had Charles followed these suggestions for successful communicating, his marriage would have been laid on a much more secure footing.

Be clear about your own needs and feelings. If Charles needed time alone to feel less burdened with the responsibilities of marriage, he could have explained that to Liz.

Think carefully through the fears or self-imposed expectations that often block openness in communicating. These need to be eliminated. Understanding old insecurities is like turning on a light at night—it dispels the ghostlike shadows of those old feelings.

Discuss those needs and feelings thoroughly with your loved one. Gaining each other's understanding and support, instead of creating suspicion and pain, takes persistent efforts.

An open, confident attitude communicates safety regarding your love. Doing too many things alone, by choice, is risky at best, but failing to share those experiences, or discuss the reasons, creates anxiety and is likely to result in retaliation.

Role expectations. Our society has slowly but surely developed a catalog of role expectations for men and women. Some of these are needed in order to define masculinity and femininity, and to help us with our identities. Many of them, however, are false and misleading.

Charles, like many men, felt that he had to be strong. And his definition of being strong was to be independent. He believed he had the right to do as he pleased, and that he was accountable to no one—not even his wife.

Now the truth of the matter was that Charles had a mother who was quite overprotective and often extremely harsh. In order to become separated from her domination, he had silently gone about his own activities and successfully concealed many of them from her. Unconsciously, he was practicing those old habits with his wife. Understanding that those old habits were no longer necessary helped Charles to free himself from those damaging habits and opened up better communication.

Hiding feelings. Covering up emotions that seem unacceptable is another barrier to good communication. In my family, we were taught not to be angry, and I was never allowed to talk back to my parents.

I'm sure they did not intend to, but they created in my mind a quiet belief that I should never express my angry, aggressive feelings. I was, however, allowed to cry. Unconsciously, I developed the habit of squelching my anger, and then crying it out, often alone.

It was most difficult for me to learn to recognize and accept my anger; to express it firmly, but with control, was even more challenging. Making myself speak openly and honestly about the anger-motivating issues was a monumental task. Learning to save my tears for real sadness was another tough job.

Here are the steps I took in doing that:

1. *I accepted the fact that it was not a sin to be angry.* From people whom I respected and from a new acquaintance with biblical truth, I realized that anger can be healthy. I believed that, and began to recognize my angry feelings.

2. *I began to express my anger verbally.* As I look back, I now suspect that I was quite obnoxious about those expressions, but I'm grateful I took that risk. Gradually, I learned to speak with more control, while staying honest.

3. *I practiced keeping my inner feelings, my words, and my body language congruent.* I once had cried when I was angry. Now I allow my face to look stern, and I suspect my eyes flash the intensity of my emotion. I rarely yell, but I know my voice is strong. No one could now be confused about whether I am sad or angry!

4. *I practiced my invaluable triad:* (a) verbalize how you feel; (b) discover why you feel it; and (c) decide what you will do about it. These worked wonders!

Please review your own beliefs about your repertoire of emotions. Understand that all emotions and needs are acceptable, and must not be denied or hidden. The more you understand and accept all of your feelings, the more alive and strong you will be. It is, of course, essential that you express such facets of your being clearly and verbally, as well as through actions, gestures, and facial expressions. Even your tone of voice is a most important means of communicating feelings.

Commit yourself to openly, honestly, and appropriately sharing any need or feeling you have with each other.

Silence, the widest of all communication gaps. Getting in touch with one's feelings is usually a painful process. Rediscovering old hurts and recognizing that pain may be a truly agonizing process.

I sometimes compare this process, however, to the lancing of an abscess.

I once had such an infection around a tooth. It throbbed and ached for some time before I could get it attended to. I shall never forget the excruciating pain, as the dentist incised that abscess. But I remember the blessed relief when the intolerable pressure was relieved.

It is the pain of the lancet that, I believe, keeps people silent about their needs and feelings. They are familiar with the chronic throb of their emotional ailments, and they even may become so accustomed to it that they are unaware of the ache.

Failure to face the pain, however, means the harboring of potentially deadly germs. An abscess may erode into blood vessels, causing septicemia (blood poisoning) and possible death.

Exactly such a thing may happen to your lovely new marriage, if you fail to learn to be open about communicating. Sooner or later, the germs of doubt, distance, and interpersonal coldness will do their deadly work.

Please don't wait for that! Seek professional help if you need it, but do not settle for silence!

Unfavorable Comparisons

Janice had not dated many boys or men during her school years, but there had been two or three whom she liked a lot. It was Joe, however, who finally captivated her. His romancing had just the right touch, and she fell deeply in love with him. There were a few episodes during their engagement that troubled her— a touch of cruelty, a recurrent need for the admiration of another girl, a hint of selfishness. She loved Joe so much, however, that she was convinced love would win out, and Joe would be different after their wedding.

Now let me remind you again: No wedding ever really changed anyone's deep personal needs or their basic personality. And Joe did not change. Janice's expectations that he would change, in fact, seemed to aggravate his problems.

As disappointments built and disenchantment ensued, Janice found herself thinking, *I know Roger or Kevin would not be like Joe. Perhaps I made a mistake.*

For weeks she tormented herself with such unfavorable comparisons. One day she happened to see Roger on the street. He had become fat and looked unkempt. Out of her shock, Janice discovered an important fact. There is no perfect person. Certainly Joe had his faults, but she could tolerate those with better grace than the flaws she saw so quickly in Roger.

Unfavorable comparisons are inevitable. Just be sure that you compare the total picture, not just the problem areas. A friend of mine says that on a perfection scale of one to ten, few people could score more than six or seven. If you traded one spouse for another, you would get a different set, but you would end up with only a six or seven.

Making the most of who you are and the person you chose is far superior to finding fault and wishing you could trade her (him) in. Do not allow yourselves to continue shopping after you have made your decision.

Inferiority Feelings

Finding balances in life is a constant challenge. That fact is apparent in the issue of balancing humility with self-esteem. Somewhere in the process of establishing that balance, a great many people end up feeling sadly inadequate. They see almost everyone else as better than they are. Such people cannot accept a compliment. They are quick to believe that they are unattractive, incompetent, and undesirable.

Such feelings create problems in all relationships, but they are especially damaging in a marriage. They set the stage for painful criticisms and slavish submission to increasing domination by the spouse.

Lori and Ron evidenced this problem. Ron was debonair and socially at ease anywhere, while Lori was shy and most uncomfortable with more than a few close friends. She would cling to Ron at parties, and he came to feel so burdened by her that he deeply resented taking her with him. The more irritated he became, of course, the more inadequate Lori felt, and the more she would cling. Within only a few months of their wedding, their marriage was almost destroyed by her inferiority feelings.

You can love others only as you love yourself. And when you feel inferior, you are not loving and accepting yourself unconditionally. It is a paradox, but as you learn to feel really loving, and act so toward yourself as well, you will be able to love your spouse all the more. And as you balance tender love with tough love, you will stop your spouse from unfair domination or controls that will sooner or later spoil your masterpiece.

Jealousy—Constructive and Destructive

One of the most common destroyers of happiness in marriage is jealousy. Few indeed are spouses who have never felt its stab. And yet the Bible, especially the Old Testament, is replete with references stating that God is a jealous God (Exodus 20:5; Ezekiel 39:25; Zechariah 1:14 are a few examples).

The following insights will help clarify the differences between godly jealousy and its destructive counterpart.

God, being all wise and all loving, knows that unswerving allegiance to Him will bring to His followers the highest joy and fulfillment possible. He craves, therefore, such single-minded devotion, knowing that anything else will bring eventual pain and damage.

Destructive jealousy, on the other hand, emanates from weakness and a sense of inferiority—quite the opposite to the strength of God's loving jealousy. Furthermore, negative jealousy expresses itself in retaliation, manipulation, or whining pleas. The jealous spouse is likely to seek his own interests from other women, hurt the real or imagined lover of his wife, or scheme to catch them in the act. Such maneuverings can, and often do, transmute something really innocent into a full-blown affair. It is certain to crystallize doubts and further estrangement.

If your relationship is threatened by jealousy, try these ideas to stop that threat.

First of all, study yourself. Be honest. Do you really feel inadequate and fear that another person is a potential rival? If so, why? Certainly others may have abilities or looks you don't have, but you have gifts they will never have. Furthermore, your loved one chose you from all those others, so he or she must have loved you. Rest in that love—it is not just from your sweetheart's goodness! It is deserved by you!

Next, evaluate your spouse. It is possible that he or she is allowing a really dangerous situation to develop without realizing it. In as loving and calm but firm manner as possible, sit down and describe the facts as you see and hear them. Offer to talk together with your clergyman or a counselor, either to relieve your fears or to help your spouse recognize and admit the risks and eliminate them.

Next, as you learn to feel secure about yourself, you may be relieved to know the whole so-called affair was an exaggeration of your imagination. This (your imagination) you can control, so you need never feel jealous again.

If there is unfaithfulness on the part of your loved one, however, your charity, love, and firmness can often stop it.

If your "loved one" does not, in fact, love you, and is unwilling to learn to do so, perhaps the earlier you discover that, the better. You can then come to a logical decision about your loss, grief, and personal healing.

Spiritual Spoilers

It is amazing to me that the highest area of our lives can so readily become the source of difficulty. The area of spiritual life and growth should draw together a couple in the glow of God's divine love and wisdom. Instead, here are a few things that can go awry!

Priorities become disarranged. While God certainly deserves the first place on your priority list, strangely He never competes with other items. Instead He flows into them with His love and joy, wisely making them all work smoothly together.

What does seem to happen, however, is the replacement of God by *religious legalities.* When church meetings and activities crowd out time for one another and create rivalry and then resentments, count on it, God is no longer at the head of your list.

On a regular basis, I strongly plead with you, check out your time allotment and the focus of your interest. If these are disproportionately directed away from your loved one and your home, revise your priorities!

The Church has become grievously divided over bigger and smaller philosophies and directions. Sooner or later such divisions will invade your marriage, if you let them. One or the other is likely to get caught up in proving your point of view and determinedly setting about making the other wrong. Such power struggles may be cloaked in self-righteousness that sounds spiritual but may be a holier-than-thou attitude. You can see how destructive such situations will inevitably become.

Secular life, with its many demands, on the other extreme, is a constant magnet, drawing busy people away from spiritual values and growth. When this begins to happen, it is subtle and disguised as responsibility, fatigue, or a super self-confidence that denies the need of God's help.

When jobs or other interests dislodge God from His place in your life, however, you and your marriage will be in jeopardy. You will believe you no longer need to read His Word. You have heard it all your life, haven't you? Why join a Bible study or spend precious time on your own to review all that?

Next, your *prayer time* is likely to be curtailed. After all, you can pray on the run. God hears you anywhere, doesn't He? Certainly so, but you are likely to be focusing on where you are going rather than on His presence. You are likely to become too tired for church services. Surely God would rather you took care of your body, and you can hear a service on TV or the radio.

Another God? As you insidiously stray away from God, you will inevitably replace His function in your life with another god. Money, perhaps power, position, hobbies, or any number of good, indifferent, or bad things will certainly take His place. You may unconsciously feel some guilt and act irritable, but you may come to a place where you will hardly miss Him.

If you do not lose yourself in too much busyness for God, it is likely you will be tempted and drawn away from Him. Either extreme is almost sure to damage—if not destroy—your marriage.

God is love, and love is God. Without Him, your only reliable resource for a whole and healthy life is missing. Keep your priorities in order, and God as the center of your life as well as your marriage.

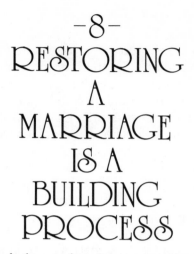

–8–
RESTORING
A
MARRIAGE
IS A
BUILDING
PROCESS

In the Foreword, the marks of a masterpiece were described, and I pointed out the magnificence of the ocean as an example of the genius of the Creator.

I am acutely aware of His mastery of all areas of life, and His ability to redeem good out of the worst of circumstances. Out of the awesome, seemingly destructive power of storms, emerges the peace that can be valued only because of the contrast. Thunderstorms clear the air of impurities, and the electricity of the lightning creates nitrates that enter the soil by way of the rain, fertilizing it.

Even greater peace and harmony settle upon the world in the wake of Nature's storms. Because God is the Master Designer, exactly that peace can be restored after your interpersonal storms. Here are some of the powerful restorers of the perfection of your masterpiece.

An Understanding Heart

It takes *information, time,* and *willingness* to acquire understanding. An elderly friend once told me a story of her childhood that taught me an invaluable lesson.

This lady was routinely critical; she rarely smiled and never cried. While I respected her capabilities, I found it impossible to love her as warmly as I wished. She related this episode one day when I was busy, but fortunately I found the time to listen.

She had lost her mother at the birth of a younger sister. She and her sister had gone to live with relatives, but in the course of time, her father remarried and took the younger child back into his home, where there were several other playful, happy children. My friend, whom I'll call Sarah, always believed that she, too, would return to live with that noisy, happy family.

When Sarah was almost seven, her father came to visit her. Knowing from a letter that he would be there prompted her to believe that this was the time she would return home with him. Carefully she packed everything she could into her valise and eagerly awaited his arrival.

Sure enough he came! Sarah had expected him to come in the wagon or surrey, but the fact that he was riding his big, black horse didn't really worry her. She was so excited to be going home at long last!

After a visit, Sarah's father rose to leave. Anxiously now, she said, "Wait a minute, Daddy, I have to get my bag."

Her father's answer made her panic. "What bag, Sarah?" She knew, then, that he would not take her home. Nevertheless she begged, cried, and even clung in terror to the foreleg of his horse, desperately pleading to go home.

Not knowing how else to handle her, Sarah's father flicked her with his riding crop, making her release her grip on the horse, and rode away. That day, Sarah said, she decided it did no good to cry. She vowed that she would never cry again and resolutely resigned herself to years of loneliness and rejection.

At the conclusion of Sarah's story, I understood her critical, reserved personality. Our tears mingled as I hugged her with a genuine warmth I had never before felt for her.

It is through such communication that understanding is made complete.

You must understand yourselves and each other if you are to

restore and build your marriage before and after the wedding night. The more you share of your childhood's joys and pain, the better you can, as I did with Sarah, truly understand each other. Here are some other helps.

Truth Is Distorted by Emotions

Anger vs. truth. A major misunderstanding I encounter in counseling is this: "What is said in anger is the *real* truth." This is not only a misunderstanding, it is frank misinformation—simply not valid. What people say in anger is a blind, unconscious conglomeration of feelings and half-truths that are designed to hurt one's opponent. What could be further from the truth? Do not believe that assumption.

Not only does anger distort the truth but so do fatigue and illness. When you are exhausted or suffering from the flu, the entire world is likely to seem unfriendly and you will believe the worst of anyone.

Anger vs. pain. Remember that pain and anger are Siamese twins, so closely attached that one cannot live without the other. Hold off your anger until you can define your pain—or that of your sweetheart. Deal with the pain through information, caring, and forgiving. Most of the time, you will discover the anger is gone. You will not need to get even, and a vicious cycle will be prevented.

Echoes from old tapes. When a husband criticizes his wife, it is rarely only a here-and-now event. She is almost certain to feel (usually unconsciously) some of the sadness of her childhood and perhaps the times when her mother or father criticized the carelessness of her work. If you will only understand how much of your present response to your mate belongs to him or her, you will deal with that very well. But when that is stacked upon unresolved issues from your past, you are almost certain to overreact, causing confusion and further pain.

You Can Rule Your Emotions

So many times I have said, "You make me so sad [hurt, or angry]!" And I believed that! In fact, unwittingly I gave people power over my emotions, and I did not know how to change that —but I learned how!

Such a change can happen to you. It comes about through *insight and understanding*. No matter how real and intense they are, you can control your feelings, rather than allowing them to rule you. Now do not deny, hide, or play games with your feelings. But do find out what they are all about:

1. Name your feelings, and you will at once be less at their mercy. Your mind is coming back into control.

2. Explain them. By knowing what past or present events prompted them, you are even closer to resolving them.

3. Determine what you will do about the situation and the emotions and then *do* it.

4. Finally, let go of the whole thing, just as you dropped the handkerchief in the old game you played as a child.

It is your God-given capacity to make choices that give you the ultimate power over life's problems. You can choose to understand, control, and work through problems and the feelings that surround them, or you can fall apart, succumbing to the stresses of life.

Sublimation

This is a word you will recognize as related to *sublime,* meaning extremely blissful or lovely. It is, in fact, an almost forgotten psychiatric word, and it is extremely important that you understand it. *Sublimation is the process of taking a potentially negative situation and turning it into something beautiful.*

One example is related to your sexual adjustment. Each of us has a measurable (or limited) amount of energy for all of our life's activities. As mentioned before, we need to budget that carefully, so as to save enough for loving through sexual intimacy. There are times, however, when that is impossible for some reason. We may be ill, unusually pressured at work, or suffer some injury that can limit or even permanently handicap sexual activity.

It is in such times or situations that the spouse who may be deprived of sexual fulfillment needs to understand sublimation. He or she can deliberately use that sexual energy for other useful and creative purposes. In teaching or working with children, for example, one may give much affection and get that in return. Making music, instrumental or vocal, can also express feelings and substitute in part for sexual expression. You can find your own individual means of burning up the energy that you may not be able, for a time, to use as you would like.

Another most important use of sublimation is related to anger. Being angry can so quickly inoculate fear into your relationship. Anger is the result of emotional pain, and all too often it ends up inflicting pain in return.

Growing up on a farm taught me many things, and one of those pearls of wisdom was the demonstration of the instinct to *retaliate*. Baby chicks were fed carefully prepared cereal bits, and there were plenty of pieces for all of them. I used to watch them busily pecking away, and I always found that sooner or later, two chicks would want the same piece of food. One would peck at the other in order to push it away from the coveted grain. The other would promptly return the peck, and soon a real fight would develop. Only the authoritative intervention of the mother hen would stop such a fight, though she rarely bothered about that, and allowed her chicks to establish their own pecking order.

Children are much like baby chicks. They, too, seem instinctively to hit back. Such childhood habits do not disappear as we grow older. In fact, they continue right on and become part of the spoiling of marital bliss in refined (and usually less physical) ways.

The wonderful answer to this predicament lies in the learning of the art of sublimation. Healthy maturity involves the willingness to give up childish instincts and replace them with adult practices. You can learn to recognize the painful frustrations that make you want ever so intensely to get even. And you can stop yourself from doing so. You can even learn to do something constructive about the situation that prompted such anger. Using the energy you may have spent in retaliation to solve problems in a loving and positive way—*that* is sublimation.

I hope you can see how this skill will consistently restore the perfection of your marital masterpiece. Practice this regularly, and you will experience its benefits. You do need to understand, however, that this is a skill, and it will not come easily to you. Going against any instinct is extremely difficult.

Let me illustrate that fact. When I was in medical school, I learned how to diagnose certain illnesses from the study of blood cells. In order to acquire those tiny cells, of course, I had to get a few drops of blood. Guess where I had to acquire them! No, not from a suffering patient, but from my own finger. I was given a tiny lancet that I had to insert into my own finger deeply enough to allow a few drops of blood to flow.

Even now I wince as I recall those experiences. My right hand held the instrument and my left hand was poised, ready for the stab. As the lancet descended, my left hand jerked away, instinctively recoiling from the pain of that sharp stab. My right hand had quite a chase, I can tell you.

I learned then what I am trying to teach you now. I disciplined myself, through the sheer power of my will, to hold that left hand absolutely still and to make it submit to the pain of the lancet. Making yourself give up the instinct to retaliate is exactly like learning to hold that hand still. It is painful, difficult, and takes a strong will. The results make it all worthwhile.

Forgiveness

When there is a rift between you and your loved one, you are certain to feel uneasy or even acutely distressed. If you have been the offender, you will feel guilty and afraid of your loved one's anger. The loss of warmth and intimacy will be threateningly cold. You will crave forgiveness.

Now you may honestly intend to forgive, and even say those words, but their reassuring quality will be missing—unless you have achieved the deep understanding described above.

Take the time to listen and talk together about each hurt you feel. Whether the pain is big or little, rare or frequent, it deserves attention. When you least feel like it, you need to do this the very most. As you discuss your misunderstandings, be attuned to the other's needs, which prompted the unwitting infliction of pain, and try to help him or her to understand that need.

When you are the victim of pain, you will not feel at all like reaching out to help your persecutor. It does, however, make sense to ask this of you, because doing so will prevent more pain later on.

Susan was extremely hurt and frightened when her fiancé showed more than a friendly interest in a girl who worked in his office. She tried to reason away his evident infatuation, but a friend reported that she had seen the two of them in a risky situation.

Hurt though she was, Susan lovingly confronted Ed. As they talked, it became clear to her that he was nervous about assuming the responsibilities of their approaching marriage. Feeling inadequate, he had unconsciously been vulnerable to the flirtatious ways of his co-worker. In a burst of insight, Ed was able to listen to Susan, as she told him what she suspected to be the cause of that little but dangerous fling. The two of them went to a counselor and worked with her to achieve the security and trust they needed for building a marriage.

You will recognize, of course, that Susan was exceptionally

secure and mature. But you can all grow toward that and can practice just that same set of skills. Through confronting in love, listening with the heart, and a thorough understanding of why Ed had his little detour, Susan could truly forgive him and help him grow into greater maturity of his own.

Forgiving in its best form demands:

1. Looking through the act to its motivation.
2. Understanding the needs and feelings that are such motivation.
3. Finding positive means for meeting those needs and expressing those feelings.
4. Working to break the old negative habits and forming new, healthy patterns.

Information About Needs

As two adults who are young, love each other deeply, and are intensively involved with getting a home and financial security established, you may not philosophize very profoundly. Try to lay aside those more vital issues for a moment. This is what each of you must have in order to adjust successfully and get your personal needs met.

Only when your needs are met can your emotions be positive enough to result in that incomparable sense of well-being you crave. It is, in fact, from this sense that the energy flows which allows you to function well.

When those needs are not recognized and met, there will develop a sense of uneasiness. You will feel anxious, and may behave in an irritable manner. You are almost certain to act out those needs in strange and indirect ways that may not result in successfully meeting them.

Here, then, is a review of those needs that I have found most useful in my own life.

Affection. Everyone needs to feel loved. We need this to be unconditional—the acceptance of us exactly as we are with warmth and tenderness. Affection is more clearly defined as the communication of such love and acceptance. This needs to be physical, verbal, and honest. Some people call the demonstration of affection "positive strokes." Whatever you call it, just do it. Not only do you need to give affection but you must have it as well. In fact, I urge you not to give more than you have.

The sources of your own need for affection are several, and you need never want for an endless source of love. I recommend that you start by getting intimately in touch with God, who *is* love. His love flows through me at times, even when I don't even feel especially loving, but He also loves me—and you! So do cultivate a sense of His nearness and allow His love to be yours.

Next, be able to ask for affection from your relatives and friends. This sort of love is not sexual, but it is comforting and warm. Be sure to ask for it when you need it! Many people believe that needing to ask detracts from the value of affection. That is an absolutely false concept. People cannot read your mind, have needs of their own, and they may not have any way of realizing your need. However, they would be not only willing but also anxious to give you a hug, a word of encouragement, or whatever you need.

When you have a reservoir full of such broad affection, you will be less desperate about your needs being met totally by your sweetheart or spouse. Remember that needing too much, and being overly dependent, can create a burden for your loved one and a strain in your relationship.

The best and most enjoyable source of affection on a human level is your spouse or sweetheart. The depth of your intimacy should mean that, after marriage at least, there is total freedom to ask, receive, offer, and give almost limitlessly to each other. Be sure to work at making this so.

Approval. While love and affection need to be unconditional, approval is quite the opposite. In order to feel pride in anyone, that person must merit such an emotion. In order to be attracted to each other at all, I know you felt admiration and approval about some qualities. As you came to know each other better, no doubt you discovered more admirable qualities. And as you did see a few troublesome areas, you tended to gloss over them with the magic of your love.

As you get to know each other better, however, those trouble spots may become friction rubs of real pain. What are you to do with these in order to give and get the approval each of you needs? You see, this is the source of real vulnerability.

If she no longer thinks he is handsome and begins to disapprove of his enlarging girth, he may turn to another woman who likes big men. Or, if he feels that she is not exciting as a luncheon companion, she may be tempted to meet another man for lunch. It is out of just such tiny beginnings that big marital explosions develop. Don't take risks!

There are only three positive options for meeting your need of approval:

1. Consistently express the approval and pride you honestly feel in your sweetheart.

2. In a positive, loving, and constructive manner discuss the qualities that trouble you about your mate and offer specific means of correcting them. Ask your partner for suggestions and, of course, develop a plan together.

3. If your partner cannot or will not try to correct these problems, put on your selective "blinders." Love him or her for those original strengths that drew you together, and choose to ignore the few problems that continue to exist.

In today's stressful and pleasure-seeking world, be aware of your temptation to take a fourth option that is highly destructive. That option, for many, has been separation and divorce. *(If he or she does not please me and make me happy, I will simply leave. There must be a better person in this world who will be more to my liking, so I will search till I find her [or him].)* Such shortsightedness is likely to result in a revolving door with ever-intensifying disenchantments and renewed searches.

The basic difficulty with this option is that the focus on problem solving is directed externally. The blame is on the other person, and unconsciously that prevents one's taking a look inside. *What is there about me that feeds into and aggravates this friction? How can I learn, grow, and change through struggling with the issue to a positive conclusion? Could I become a more mature person by accepting some bottom-line, unchangeable limits?* I believe the answer to both questions is, "Yes!"

Predictability. When I was little, I frequently became upset over conflicts with my siblings and my mother. Because they were the source of my pain, I did not know how to go to them for comfort or solutions. I was most fortunate, however, to have a quiet, peaceful, and unconditionally accepting grandmother. She lived with us, and in her room was a soft bed on which there was the softest coverlet I ever felt.

How often I retreated to that room! Grandmother would be sitting in her rocking chair sewing, and she would look at me over her glasses as I threw myself, sobbing, on her bed. Burying my face in her soft blanket, I could cry out my childish frustrations as long and intensely as I needed to. All my grandmother ever said was a soft Pennsylvania Dutch word, *"Oi! Oi!"* I don't know, even now, what that word meant, but I know it comforted me, and best of all, that comfort was there for me every time I needed it. My grandmother was predictable. I could count on her.

Even when another person is not as comforting as my grandmother, if he reacts in reasonably the same manner in a given type of situation, one can cope successfully. It is the inconsistency of responses to the same sort of need stimulus that creates problems.

Learn with each other, then, to respond as kindly and lovingly as you can. If you must exhibit disapproval or irritation over certain issues, however, at least do so every time you feel it. And use those frustrations to resolve the problems and grow in your interpersonal adjustments.

Congeniality. Part of loving and showing affection to each other must include smiles and laughter. Merriment is so essential to personal and marital health, however, that I want to emphasize it. Being able to see the humor in tense times is a special gift.

Some people are naturally better at this than others, but everyone can develop this skill with a little effort.

Again, let me remind you to *avoid ever laughing at each other.* Laughing at your own self and together at the humorous aspects of almost any problem can relieve the tension and release you to find solutions.

Find fun in life as well as in the tense situations that need humor for their resolution. Look for jokes that are worth sharing. When you read, share the funny ideas with your loved one. And sometimes, laugh just for the joy of it. "A merry heart doeth good like a medicine," was told us thousands of years ago by Solomon (Proverbs 17:22). Modern medicine is only recently rediscovering the truth of that.

Patience

As we waited for our friends, my husband and I became nervous. Our dinner reservation was one that demanded our being on time, and we were almost certain to be late. Jean was almost never on time. Her husband, Rob, was quite the opposite, always punctual and well organized. Yet he remained calm, assuring us that Jean would be ready soon and calling the restaurant to be sure to hold the reservations open. Rob certainly had found Jean's tardiness to be an irritant over the years of their marriage, but he had chosen to practice the gracious quality of patience with her. When Jean, looking elegant, finally entered the room, Rob looked at her only with love, and we all enjoyed a pleasant evening.

I need not describe to you the opposite picture of irritation, lecturing, and even subtle disapproval that could have spoiled the evening for all of us.

How can you, like Rob, develop this elusive quality of patience? Here are some suggestions:

1. It takes trials to produce and refine patience. So the next time your spouse annoys you, consider the possibility of turning that annoyance into an opportunity to practice

being patient. I suspect most of you will have tried scolding, begging, and even bullying that slow spouse into punctuality without success, anyway. So now try learning to live lovingly.

2. Recall the times that you have been slow to learn, and consider what sort of treatment you would have liked. Try that out on your spouse.

3. Learn to count high, bite your tongue, relax, and simply exert the self-control that it takes to stop nagging and start being patient.

4. While you are waiting, think of the good qualities of your mate. By the time he or she has finally done the job, mastered the lesson, or is ready for your date, you can feel truly loving rather than angry.

Excellence in Communication

Over a cup of coffee one evening, Dan was relating his schedule to his wife, Meg. He listed several appointments over the next few days and then said, "And Sunday afternoon, I'll be meeting with Mr. Jones about our new project." Meg often felt neglected by Dan, but this message was too much! Sunday was her birthday, and obviously Dan had not even thought of it.

Usually, Meg had tried to put Dan's plans ahead of her needs, and yet she realized that lately she had been feeling quite resentful of that. Choosing her words carefully, she asked, "By that, Dan, do I understand that you have forgotten my birthday? You know birthdays are special to me, and I feel hurt and angry that you would plan such a big meeting on my special day! I want you to know that I am going to celebrate it with my sister, and I hope you'll be able to change your plans and join us!" Fortunately Dan could, and he did.

Clear communications must define one's own feelings and needs, consider the other's, and propose a solution. Meg's handling of her situation did all of those.

Here are the best policies for effective communicating:

1. *Think carefully about the message you want to convey* to your listening spouse. Say it clearly, making certain that your tone of voice and body language match the words you say. This avoids mixed messages and misleading options. Meg could have said, "I'd rather you didn't meet Mr. Jones on my birthday." Such a statement seems to leave Rob a choice, which Meg did not honestly intend.

2. *Observe your listener's face as you speak.* If your spouse looks puzzled, surprised, or annoyed, and that expression doesn't fit the response you expected, stop talking at once! Ask your spouse what he or she heard you say, and find out if you were understood. If not, clarify your message.

3. *Listen.* Give your listener a chance to talk and give him or her the courtesy of hearing his message. The art of active listening is one I find sadly lacking in many people. It is so easy to let your thoughts wander, and to fail to develop the honestly caring attitude that really wants to hear the other out.

Listening is an attitude of one's mind and heart, not just a neurological function of the auditory system. Try hard to keep your mind open to simple facts, not just your own opinions. And remember to separate your feelings and wishes from such unreasonableness. All too often, we eagerly search for ideas that will back up our selfish wishes. We make up our minds, then we choose to not be confused with facts!

Good communications cannot be achieved until you are both willing to go beyond your own self-centeredness and honestly seek the good of both of you!

4. *Always recognize your feelings and separate them from the facts.* One of the best tools in clear communicating is to verbalize one's emotions before beginning to discuss an issue. I might say, "I feel worried about the question of buying a new car right now." The fact that I am worried

will help both me and my spouse to recognize that I need reassurance, not glib answers. Then we will be ready to discuss "How can we make any more payments, when we barely balanced our budget last month?" From there, honesty, a willingness to explore all the possible options, and a loving concern for each other's needs can achieve a positive solution.

Facts and feelings are equally important. It is the mixing of them, and the denial of emotions, that creates confusion and prevents successful communication.

Courage to confront in love. Few areas of interpersonal relationships are as difficult to address as that of confronting. On the other hand, I believe true intimacy is never achieved until people are able to disagree and express feelings directly with each other. To restore the harmony of your marriage, or to build it at all, demands expertise in confrontation.

Speak the truth in love. To confront successfully, you will have to learn to speak the truth in love. That love may be tender, or it may need to be tough, but it must be honest, kind, and open. The truth may be focused on feelings, decisions, or opinions, but you must remember that it is truth as you see it. Your spouse may take an opposite point of view and believe that is *The Truth.* So be very careful that you do not act as if your word were the law. Only God's Word is the ultimate truth, and people often twist even that to fit their arguments.

Openness. Being open to all the information you can acquire is extremely important to good confrontation. When you can hear each other out, and stay willing to modify your position, then you are ready to confront in love. You may not, in fact, end up changing your opinion, but your honest willingness to do so will be clear, and your opponent/lover will respect your open-mindedness.

Tough love. Tough love, at times, is angry—as a good parent is angry when he sees a child behaving in a way that is obnoxious or hurtful. Such a confrontation is the most difficult of all! When you see the person you love more than all others behaving or deciding erroneously, you need to tell him or her. But if you say something critical, you risk losing his affection, and your marital harmony may be sacrificed. What a dilemma!

As they drove home from a party, Steve and Gail felt estranged, and sat as far apart as their small car would permit. Jean decided that her husband needed a lesson in manners, so she launched a critique of their evening. Every phrase and gesture that had annoyed her became a coal for the flame of her anger. She ended her lecture by saying, "You embarrass me! You act like a creep, and I'm not at all sure I will ever go anywhere with you again!"

Steve became silent, fearing that whatever he might say would be wrong. He had grown up in a rural area and was not very socially skilled. His wife's denouncements hit where it hurt the most. Had she realized his self-doubts in this vulnerable area, she could have said something like this: "Steve, I really like the way you smiled at people this evening. I could tell they liked you. Do you mind if I tell you one little thing you do that bothers me? Once in a while, you talk with food in your mouth. Do you think you could remember not to do that? Or could I remind you by touching your hand?" What a difference such an approach could make!

Peace at all costs. When one spouse, like Gail, is easily upset, the other may become excessively patient and placating. Some people seek peace at any cost, but unfortunately, that cost may be too high. Peace-at-any-cost people actually become dishonest in their heroic efforts to avoid arguments and anger. Over a period of time, this philosophy allows an unfair balance of power, and eventually results in disrespect and resentment.

I hope you will both learn to disagree with respect and intelligence, working through your points of view to a fair compromise. Respecting each other as people, like unconditional love, is independent of opinions and feelings. It is a decision to be made and a discipline to be practiced.

Honesty

When both of you have learned to be kind, patient, and forgiving, it will not be hard to be honest. Most dishonesty emanates from fear of the loved one's disapproval and rejection.

Honesty is built on trust. Being open and honest becomes easy if your spouse does not betray your frankness. You can afford to admit downright mistakes as well as poor judgments, when you can count on your spouse to understand and forgive.

Kathy had one very risky habit—she drove too fast, and at times was a bit careless. As she drove home one summer day, she was preoccupied with plans for the evening, and failed to see the stoplight turn red. As she realized that she had to stop quickly, her foot slipped off the brake, and she hit the car ahead of her, damaging its taillights severely. She was not hurt, and both cars were drivable. How she dreaded telling George! Her father had terrified her years before by his anger over a teenage fender-bender, and she was certain her husband would also be harsh with her.

Anxiously, Kathy awaited her husband's homecoming. She chose to tell him about her accident at once, so she could get his anger over with as soon as possible. When he entered the house, she knew that he had seen the damaged car but, to her surprise, instead of anger she saw tenderness and concern. He touched her gently and asked if she was hurt. He then listened as she recounted the episode, even being honest about her driving too fast and being inattentive.

Carefully, George asked her about the details of reporting the accident and gaining information for their insurance. Then he took her gently into his arms and held her, while her tears of release from her fear rolled down her face. He softly assured her that cars could be mended or replaced, but that she could not. As he reaffirmed his love, Kathy realized how blessed she was, and her love for George grew incredibly that evening. Furthermore, she vowed to correct her driving habits. What a restorer of marital harmony! What a masterpiece their marriage!

Not only is it vital to be honest about facts and events but it is also essential that you be honest about your feelings! Be honest when you are excited and happy, and be just as sincere when you are worried, afraid, hurt, or angry.

You men, I suspect, have the hardest job when it comes to emotional honesty. Our world teaches you to be strong, courageous, and *in charge* at all times. And yet there are times when you feel weak and are worried. You, too, would like to lean on someone for a while.

Let me urge you to be honest with your spouse about all of your feelings. You need not be maudlin and certainly you must share such vulnerable areas in your own way and time—but do risk sharing them.

Just as men have trouble expressing tender feelings, so do you wives often find it difficult to admit your angry, aggressive feelings. For many years I was unaware of feeling angry, because I had been taught as a child that it was wrong to be angry. Instead, I recognized hurt and shed tears. Now certainly anger and hurt go together, but to deal only with the hurt and never the anger was dishonest. In my case, that dishonesty was unconscious.

Many men and women, however, are not as unaware as I was about their hidden feelings. They know them very well, and deliberately use them to manipulate other people. To build or restore the harmony of your marriage, you must get rid of such manipulation. It will destroy trust, reduce respect, and create power struggles. Keep your feelings honest, and keep them separate from your intellectual functioning. Think about and resolve your needs and feelings, and then get on with your decision making.

Grace—Unmerited Favor

Lance will never forget that Saturday! He came home from work tired and anxious to spend a restful evening with his wife.

They had been married only a few years, and he still felt the thrill of greeting her. Today, however, there were guests, and the tension between them and his wife was heavy. Dave and Vickie, the guests, were Lance and Beth's friends.

The conversation of the next hour became an unbelievable blur of accusations that his lovely wife had been secretly seeing their friend Dave. Lance was sure it was not true. This had to be the fabrication of a jealous wife. He assured those friends that they needn't worry, because he and Beth were so much in love, nothing could come between them. After an eternity, the friends left. Only then did Lance let himself know the truth. Beth had, in fact, been having an affair with Dave. She had been flattered by his attentions, and allowed herself to slide into a relationship that got out of hand. She was sorry and begged Lance to forgive and trust her.

After some hours of anguish and reflection, Lance chose to forgive her. He did understand her insecurity and vulnerability, and he decided to put the entire tragic event behind them. He broke their relationship with Dave and his wife, renewed his attentions to Beth, and never brought up the subject again.

In my opinion, Lance lived out the quality of grace. Beth had betrayed him and admitted that. But instead of leaving her, Lance forgave her, loved her more tenderly, and refused to use her sin to gain power over her.

I hope none of you have such a heartbreaking crisis in your marriages. However, you are likely to go through other episodes that need the grace of understanding and forgiving. Such grace, I believe, comes from God Himself. Don't fear asking Him for it when you need it!

Wisdom

Wisdom is the ability to apply knowledge to everyday-life situations. Recognizing the habit patterns of your life, and that of your spouse, can enable you to understand them and solve the problems these habits may create.

With a sigh of relief, Joyce snuggled in the strong arms of her husband, Eric. They had just been discussing a chronic pattern of disharmony in their marriage. For a long time, Joyce had struggled with her feelings of unworthiness. She felt ugly, incapable, and often unloved. Despite those feelings, she was highly successful.

It was in the area of criticism that Joyce had such difficulty. Her husband was a positive, optimistic person but he was also direct and honest. Not realizing her sensitivity, he would express opinions and share ideas that were often contrary to hers. Joyce unconsciously took these as put-downs of her ideas, and over the months they had been married, was feeling more and more rejected. Despite trying harder to please Eric, it seemed she was never going to make it.

One evening she decided to talk it all out with her husband. She explained the hurts of her growing-up years, and how her mother's protectiveness and her father's criticism had trapped her in feeling inadequate and helpless. As they talked, Eric suddenly recognized her feelings about his openness, and she understood that she was no longer a child, trapped in her parents' mistakes.

With these insights, Joyce and Eric were able to work out a plan. He would watch her face for the telltale signs of distress and tell her about them. Joyce then would stop and separate her old feeling habits from the present, and would realize that Eric spoke from love. She could profit from his ideas, though she did not have to agree with them.

Joyce and Eric discovered wisdom—the ability to put insight and information to work in solving daily problems of life.

Realism

As I examined Peggy, the new baby of one of my most lovable families, she began to cry. In only a few seconds, her pink cheeks turned pale, then dusky. Her cry was hoarse. Peggy had been born with a heart defect, and the slightest exertion caused the unoxygenated blood from her tissues to mix with that from her lungs. The mixed blood had a dark color that made her look dusky. Worst of all, she was weak due to the inadequate oxygen supply, and she would never be able to run and play as her friends would.

I will never forget the tender care Peggy's family showered upon her. Realizing her limitations, they loved her all the more, and wisely encouraged her to do all that she could, but protected her when that became necessary.

Peggy and that special family became an object lesson that can help you in your marriage adjustments.

In our romantic Western culture, children are taught from infancy that the young man takes his bride from her wicked stepmother, and they go off to his castle to live happily ever after. The supposition is that such bliss simply happens to people with no effort.

We learn such idealism from books full of fairy tales, from romantic stories, and from the movie and TV industries. We talk of "falling" in love as if one blunderingly fell in a pond, and we hear such phrases as "This [falling in love] is bigger than the two of us!"

It is my experience that such ideas set up a great many couples for a major time of disenchantment. When she realizes he has bad breath in the morning, and he first sees her hair in curlers, the letdown begins. It continues when she has her pouting times, and he his shouting spells. Each is likely to feel he or she has been deceived or cheated!

It is at such a moment that realism needs to be put to use. The imperfection of each other's humanness must be accepted, just as Peggy's family accepted her physical problems. Such acceptance must be "because of" and not "in spite of" those flaws if it is to be credible.

It is, in fact, a great relief to know that one does not have to be perfect. And when you can realize that for yourself, you will be able to allow such freedom for your spouse.

Now let me warn you! It is easy to use this idea to make excuses for some highly annoying or even destructive habits. Such habits need to be recognized, and you must work to break them and replace them with loving ways. But do avoid starry-eyed idealism that unconsciously expects perfection, and then feel angry and hurt when reality falls short of that.

Realism can be decorated with idealism, but avoid the reverse. Your ideals keep you stretching and growing, but you must live daily in the realities of your own world.

Faith

All evening, Rick had noticed that his wife, Marie, had been talking with his friend John. John was a quiet man, and Marie seemed to be able to get him to talk more than usual. The party was fun, but Rick had to admit that he felt afraid—and just a bit jealous.

Rather than pretend such feelings did not exist, Rick talked about them with Marie. As he watched her open face, however, he felt reassured even before she spoke. She explained to him that she, too, often felt shy and was quiet, and she recognized those traits in John. She found that he was really very intelligent and had a quiet sense of humor. As they talked, he opened up more, and soon was mixing with the others at the party.

It took faith in his wife and their relationship for Rick to risk opening up his feelings. He was rewarded by her reassurance that John was not a rival for her affections.

Rick also had faith in himself. He knew that he was a good husband, and that his love for Marie was genuine. His self-confidence, of course, was somewhat lacking, or he would not have felt threatened by John. But let's face it! Most of us are threatened by our imperfections at times.

We also must have faith in God and His wisdom.

Early in my marriage, there were some traits in my husband that caused me considerable distress. I'm sorry to say that I chided and eventually nagged him about those. One weekend there was to be a special seminar in our church, and the topic of the evening session was about that area of friction between us.

My husband really did not want to attend that session, but I coerced him, and reluctantly he went with me. Just as the lecture began, a call came that took my husband away on an emergency.

As I sat alone, I heard little of that lecture for a few minutes. I felt really angry at God for allowing that emergency to take him away from the session. In all of His power and wisdom, didn't God know how much Herb needed that lecture? And why couldn't He have delayed that emergency for one hour?

A quiet thought drew my attention back to the lecture. *Perhaps it is you who need to hear this. If your husband had been here, you would have thought only of his problems and might have missed what is in it for you!* As I tuned in, I did hear ideas that I still find useful in my life.

Faith in God and His infinite wisdom is so essential to a harmonious marriage. Be sure to seek His guidance with an open mind, and accept it unquestioningly. He loves you both, and you can entrust each other and your own selves to Him!

Trust

Trust is much like faith, but perhaps it is a bit more tangible. I have faith in the things I cannot see and do not understand. I trust the laws of physics and the things I do understand. It is the consistency and predictability of life that creates the climate of trust.

I have a family who are always there for me. When I have a need or a joy, they listen and care. They do not hurt me, and they love and accept me as I am. I can trust them completely.

One of my friends is married to a man who is unskilled at household tasks. He creates more problems than he can fix when he tries to open a clogged drainpipe. She can trust him to do this —he is predictable. She has learned over many years to avoid the irritation and embarrassment it causes even to ask him for such help. She quietly calls a repairman and saves all the bad feelings.

Trust can grow only when there is unconditional love and acceptance. Such security is the essence of any successful marriage.

Congeniality

As mentioned earlier, when the writer of the Proverbs said, "A merry heart doeth good like a medicine" (17:22), he was literally thousands of years ahead of his time. Just now, medical science is becoming aware of the healing power of healthy laughter.

Every young married couple can create such an atmosphere of merriment. You need to start early, before the habits of gloom and negativism become established. *But beware of how you do it.*

When Chuck entered the house, it was like magic. His daughter ran to him for his special hug and smile. His son seemed to be waiting for his cheery greeting, and his wife felt like a light was turned on. Chuck exuded goodwill, and his cheery demeanor rarely changed. Wherever he went, Chuck created a spirit of congeniality that was contagious.

On the other hand, when Phil entered the house, his children ignored him, or found an excuse to leave as soon as possible. The difference between Phil and Chuck lay in the sort of congeniality they practiced. Chuck's was gentle and sensitive. But Phil's was thoughtless and even rude. He would tease or tickle his children until they passed the stage of laughter and became angry. His jokes often contained barbs of ridicule, and he seemed unaware of the pain his thoughtlessness caused.

Take a look at yourself. Are you able to laugh? Can you turn tension into tenderness with a loving, kind jest? Or are you too heavy in your joking? Do you lose sight of the fact that what's not fun *for* all is not fun *at* all?

Love

One of the most difficult words to define in the English language is *love.* I believe it is a mixture of all of the qualities in this chapter. It involves:

1. Understanding enough to forgive, forget, and love even more after a disagreement.

2. Patience to wait for the information that is essential to total understanding and for the healing, growing, and changing that stop pain and cultivate harmony.
3. Complete communication that includes the emotions, the intellect, and the physical aspects of a relationship.
4. Courage to overcome fears and doubts by taking the risk of confrontation.
5. Honesty and openness enough to avoid the secrets that breed doubts and fears.
6. Grace enough to give another chance, even when the loved one does not deserve it—and refusal to bring up the sins and mistakes of the past.
7. Wisdom enough to learn from one's mistakes and from the experiences of others, and hence to avoid repeating needless errors.
8. Realism enough to avoid disenchantment and to accept each other and life "as is."
9. Idealism enough to keep dreams alive and goals ahead for striving toward.
10. Congeniality enough to add the spice of wholesome laughter to every day.
11. Faith enough in oneself, one's loved one, and in God, to keep above petty jealousy or painful despair.
12. Trust enough to encourage an atmosphere of safety and honesty.
13. Love enough to encircle the two of you, as does the wedding band your finger, in endless intimacy.

Restoring sexual harmony, then, demands conquering the destroyers and cultivating the restorers. As Jesus Christ stilled the wild seas that threatened His followers, He can still the storms that will endanger your marriage. Keeping your faith in Him, in each other, and in your own self, will allow His power to penetrate every troubled situation of your lives.

–9–
MAINTAINING
A
MARRIAGE
IS A
FUN PROCESS

"What is a rose doing among my shoes?" Sherri wondered. She was home from work, and changing clothes at once was her habit. Next she opened the refrigerator and found a rose. There was another rose in the bathroom, in the cupboard when she reached for a drinking glass, and even on the TV! Altogether, Sherri discovered six roses about their new apartment—one for each week of her marriage to Tom. Surprises were already becoming a part of their marriage, but this was the happiest one yet!

"What's for dinner?" boomed Hal, as he burst into the kitchen from a long day at work. "If it can keep, put it away and let's go out for dinner. I just drove by a neat-looking restaurant, and I want to check it out!"

These two young husbands have captured the essence of fun in making a marital masterpiece that will last!

Characteristics of a Fun Marriage

In every one of us there is much of the childlike creativity of Tom and Hal. We simply have to get in touch with it, recognize its value, and put it to work.

Surprises. The element of the unexpected can keep any marriage from going stale. Surprises need not be expensive or take much time. An unexpected telephone call for no reason except to say, "I love you! I was thinking about you. How's your day?" can brighten any day for your spouse. (Now I will warn you that telephone calls on the job need to be brief and sweet.)

A special meal need not take a lot of time, only a little fore-thought and planning. Hiding the dessert until it's time to be served creates a surprise. To be a surprise, of course, means you don't do it every day!

Every couple should go out at least once a week together. In order to keep the surprise factor active in your marriage, think of some new activity to share. Taking hot dogs to a nearby park can make supper a fun event. (Do keep such outings simple, so they do not become a burden!) Going window-shopping need not cost anything, and it can be a time for dreaming of the day when you can afford a new sofa. If you can manage it now and then, a night away in a hotel or resort can be a marvelous reminder of your honeymoon.

Surprises, well planned, not too often, and lovingly carried out, will create a set of lifetime memories for both of you. What a fun marriage they will help you build!

Excitement. Surprises are exciting, but so are anticipated events. The adventurous spirit of exploring can be enhanced by planning on it, saving for it, and waiting for it.

If you can possibly do so, take a trip now and then. Perhaps it must be nearby, or perhaps, rarely, you can manage a faraway place. Collect brochures or read articles about the place you will visit. Discuss it with friends, and talk about it together. Plan all the little details of such a trip—what clothes will you take? Where will you stop for the night? Will you camp or find a motel or country inn? Allow some events to be spontaneous, but plan enough so you will experience the childlike eagerness of yearning for this special trip to take place.

Excitement is not only a big event. In almost any day, you can find the fun of excitement. It is sharing small events that can turn any day into a special, even memorable, one. A friend is getting married? A couple you enjoy are expecting a baby? The neighbors have a new puppy! If you will let yourself, you can empathize with such people, sharing their excitement with them and with each other.

Let me tell you a secret about excitement. It must be shared with feeling by both of you, if it is to be meaningful at all. Have you ever told some truly great news to someone really important to you, only to hear, "Uh-huh," or even silence? How often will you have such a response before you stop sharing your big news?

Do remember to listen to each other, and respond in interest and enthusiasm to one another's excitement. Now, of course, I must be practical. There are times when I have had such a hectic day, I simply do not have the energy for much excitement.

So will all of you have bad days and big worries, when your spouse will share some exciting news. On such occasions do the best you can to muster the strength to respond. Explain that you care and *are* interested, and that you will react more enthusiastically when you've rested a bit.

Remember, on the other hand, to save enough strength for each other. Do not very often allow your job to rob your spouse of his or her priority in your life. Fatigue is often physical, but just as often, it is a mental attitude. Do practice keeping your mental attitude positive. Love and excitement can be energy restorers if you allow that to happen!

Activity sharing. Early in my marriage I learned that my husband was a coin collector. We were both in school and had very little money, but he could occasionally find a valuable coin in the change we received in stores. He conceived the idea of writing a check for whatever we could afford, and cashing it at the bank for rolls of quarters, dimes, and nickels.

He would eagerly pore over those coins, becoming highly excited at finding one that was rare. I had to spend the coins that were not collectible for the cleaning and groceries, but eventually I got over being embarrassed about that.

I must confess there were times that I felt quite resentful of various aspects of that collecting habit. But early on, it was an activity we shared that was fun for both of us.

Activity sharing can be as broad as you like, or as narrow as it must be, but here are some specific suggestions:

1. *Each of you needs a hobby or interest of your own.* Communicate freely and negotiate clearly some boundaries for developing these individual pursuits. I urge you to set a budget that you will honestly respect. You will surely need to set a limit on the time you will each allow to be spent alone. How much time that will be depends on the two of you. Just be honest, but also remember to keep top priority for each other.

2. *The two of you need a hobby or interest that you share.* This may be an active sport such as tennis, swimming, or skiing. It may be spectator sports (if you live in an area where that is available). You may both enjoy gardening, reading, or table games. Be sure that you have the will to explore, an open mind for evaluating new experiences, and the will to stick with the process until you settle on the things you both honestly like.

3. *Keep these activities fun.* I know a couple who worked so hard to become good at tennis that they actually became angry at each other. She would blame him if they lost at doubles, and he became critical of her style. Do not allow such a negative attitude to spoil your fun.

4. *Avoid unhealthy competition.* Spurring each other on to greater skills, and celebrating successes is wonderful. But fault finding and belittling each other will soon put an end to the fun, as will gloating over the loser when you win.

5. *Be sure to laugh together.* Look for the humor in your activities and in those around you. A good laugh may be one of the best activities you share!

Frankness

Being open as well as honest is what I call *frankness*. And that is a precious but vanishing quality. In our highly competitive Western world, people learn to cover their emotions and become suspicious rather than open. Furthermore, many cultures and individuals have a belief that to demonstrate emotions openly is a weakness and not at all proper.

If you happen to be one of those people, let me urge you to review your childhood training. Retain that which is profitable and reasonable, but please discard the belief that it is wrong to feel or express certain emotions. That simply is not true. All feelings are God-given and have rightful purpose.

It is the denial or hiding of emotions that causes trouble. Likewise, it is exaggeration or explosion of emotions that makes them seem undesirable. You have already realized that surprises and excitement fall flat, when the one who is supposed to share the excitement acts bored, and the surprisee fails to be surprised!

Learn to recognize your own feelings, even when you have not been in the habit of doing so. As you become aware of your emotions, learn to express them verbally and in body language. A smile when you feel a little bit happy will enhance your good feelings. And a frown if you feel irritated will make that feeling believable.

You will find that developing the ability to know and express your own feelings will make you more sensitive to your spouse's emotions. As you both grow in this special quality, I predict that your enjoyment of each other will increase.

Yearning

The Now generation of the past two decades has had little opportunity to experience that sense of intense desire for something which I call "yearning."

When I was in high school, I yearned for a plaid, woolen skirt and soft, matching sweater, which were then the style. For several years my parents could not afford the cost of that outfit, but during my senior year the coveted skirt and sweater were finally in my wardrobe. Probably never again in my life will I experience the exquisite sensation of wearing that outfit. Had I not wanted it so intensely, of course, I could not have enjoyed it so immensely.

It is something of that caliber that I want for the two of you— a deep-seated craving for each other's presence! That yearning may, and often will be, sexual. Remember to save the time and energy to be actively responsive to one another's physical cravings. It may, as well, be emotional, social, or spiritual. In whatever area of life you feel the desire, value it. And allow it to grow to the point of truly delighting in its eventual gratification.

Let me reiterate the value of waiting for the fulfillment of your desires. When you never have to wait, you may fail to really appreciate the satisfaction of your craving. But waiting and anticipating can make your satisfaction the most complete!

Freedom With Trust

In order to find the most positive quality in the fun of your marriage, you must enjoy a certain sense of freedom. One of the finest symbols of a good marriage is that of a hand full of sand. When the hand is open it can hold a sizable mound of sand, but just closing the hand squeezes out most of it. Furthermore, with an even tighter grip, the tiny, hard grains cause friction and pain on one's skin.

Holding too tightly to each other can cause a similar loss and the pain of friction.

On the other hand, letting go too much of one another is like dropping the open hand that holds the sand. It will likewise be lost. Many marriages become so open, and the paths of each spouse so divergent, that they lose touch, and may even lose their love and marriage.

I love to travel and explore almost any new adventure. My husband, on the other hand, despises traveling and would much rather stay at home with his hobbies and TV. When our children were well established away from home, I asked him if he minded very much if I occasionally took a trip or traveled elsewhere to speak at seminars.

Frankly, he not only didn't mind but was rather glad to have me away. He was free of my expectations and needs and could do exactly as he pleased while I did my traveling.

Now such freedom is possible, I believe, only when there is honest and total trust. If I felt my husband might fall in love with another woman while I was away, I could not enjoy that freedom. And if he were afraid that I might be attracted to some other man, I think he would not enjoy his time alone.

It is always the balances that are so vital to healthy relationships. If you take each other's love for granted, you may lose it, as the fallen hand drops its sand. If you hold on too tightly you may, in a different manner, lose that precious relationship. Find your own balances, and in absolute honesty, give each other the freedom to pursue your own interests, yet retain the intimacy and sharing that make your love grow.

Above all else, I advise you to close your minds and hearts to any serious relationship with another person of the opposite sex. There are an infinity of opportunities, and if you are unaware of them, you may find yourself caught in a web you had never envisioned.

Mike noticed that Sandy's eyes were red from crying. Sandy, a co-worker, worked near him in a large office, and they often shared their morning coffee break. He quietly asked her what was troubling her, and she unburdened herself. She was troubled by her husband's drinking, and did not know how to cope.

With a kind heart and listening ear, Mike understood and comforted her. He met her after work for coffee and listened again. At first he shared Sandy's problems with his wife, but after several weeks, she grew tired of hearing about them.

Before he realized it, Mike was spending a great deal of time with Sandy, and even visited in her home. Unfortunately, this story did not end happily ever after but in a tragic divorce, and serious trouble with Sandy's jealous husband.

Too much freedom, taking one's spouse for granted, and a failure to recognize his vulnerability had cost Mike dearly!

Guard your freedom carefully, and cherish the trust that makes it possible; but do not abuse it by allowing it to become your first priority.

Fun Is Remembering

At fifty-seven, I can clearly and firmly tell you that life is for memories, just as it is for exploring. It is easy to become so busy that you fail to take the time to remember.

A noted family therapist, in fact, begins her counseling of troubled marriages by asking the couple to tell her what drew them to one another in their dating days. As they remember what made them love each other then, she can often help them recapture the glow of those experiences, and rekindle their love.

Fun is exciting and adventurous day by day. It is, even more importantly, the tender, quiet recapturing of sunsets' splendor shared, walks in a gentle spring rain, and a soft, silent moment of wordless loving. Balance your adventures with reliving the joys, and even the tears, of yesterday.

Perhaps you have the kind of mind that captures the lights and shadows of daily events and retains them. Many of us do not— and for you, I recommend building memories in a tangible way. Photographs are an obvious way of doing that, but I suggest an even more unique plan. Look for a leaf, a rock, or a wild flower or fern. Take them home and preserve them in a special box or scrapbook. A paper napkin from a party or a matchbook from a hotel can be special souvenirs of a romantic evening or a special event. Find your own individual method for remembering but *do* it! And share these memories in laughter or tenderness whenever you can.

The Fun of Silence

Intimacy grows from chatter to activity sharing, to ever deeper levels of the revealing of deep emotions and profoundly moving ideas, dreams, and experiences. It is my belief that the greatest intimacy of all is that of the unique times of silence, when thoughts and feelings can find no better expression. As you get to know one another really well, the most significant bond of all often needs no words.

While the fullness of such an experience takes years to develop, there can be moments between you when silence is more precious than words. Look for such times, trust them, and remember them. Practice the art of silence that is mellow and loving and learn to cherish that.

If you are fortunate enough to have a fireplace, plan some time to lie silently, touching one another, as you watch the flames or embers. Silence when viewing a rainbow, the majesty of mountains, or the awesome expanse of the ocean, will fix those moments in your hearts forever. Too many words may, on the contrary, release your feelings too much, and allow you to forget those special experiences.

Communication is vital. Just do not forget the power of wordlessly feeling each other's physical nearness, reveling in the warmth of that closeness, trusting the total surrender, knowing the quiet growth of ever-broadening, deepening love!

Spiritual Bonding

We talk rather glibly, these days, about psychological, emotional, social, and professional affairs. All too seldom, however, do people speak of spiritual matters. If they do, in my experience, it has become a mystical, impractical concept.

Let me remind you again that Christ compared your marriage to His ultimate relationship with His followers, the Church. So He must have intended you to know that He, at least, wants your relationship to develop spiritually, as well as physically, and in other ways.

One friend of mine told me that in her sexual relations she was most aware of the presence and blessing of Christ. How I wish that sensitivity for all of you. If you, too, can feel the joy of His nearness as completely as you sense one another in this ultimate intimacy of your love, you will begin to know true wholeness in your lives.

Spirituality really is the part of you that is most like God. The Bible tells us that "God is a Spirit: and they that worship him must worship him in spirit and in truth" (John 4:24). It is in our spirits that we can be most like Him who created us in His likeness.

Look for the priceless sense of awe at any part of God's creative masterpiece—the world, or the stars and planets. Remember that He made the perfection we often fail to notice out of nothingness. And let your spirit grow in and toward Him. If both of you will grow toward the same Being, you will find yourselves ever closer to one another as well as to Him.

In order to experience the fun process of maintaining your marriage, here are four things to remember:

1. Discover and cultivate your personal sense of congeniality and good humor.
2. Risk expressing that fun in your individual style.
3. Trust your spouse to respond to and join in your fun and remember to give that responsiveness to him or her.
4. Remember to keep the fun enjoyable for both of you, and carefully avoid laughter at the expense of the other.

By following these suggestions, I trust each of you will find and perfect the happy art of merriment as part of your marriage masterpiece!

EPILOGUE

My Prayer and Wish for You

Do you recall the introduction to this book with its description of the ocean as an example of married life? I hope you can now recognize that simile even more clearly.

It does not matter what aspects of marriage you consider—sexual, emotional, intellectual, social, or spiritual—they are the essence of your relationship as water is, the ocean. And each will vary in size, form, and intensity, as do the waves of the sea. Allow this infinite variety to challenge and intrigue you, rather than becoming confused or frustrated. As you cope with the waves, you will slowly discover that the eternal movement of the tides of your love will leave their treasures for you to cherish.

I wish for each of you a spirit of adventure and the wisdom to explore safely. Keep your loving commitment to each other fresh and express it creatively. Find excitement in growing and learning, even when at times there is pain in the process. Balance the growth and expression of your individuality with your intimacy as a couple, and you will know the maximum thrill of achievement.